Seafood

Spectacular Recipes for Every Season

Pär-Anders Bergqvist and Anders Engvall
Translated by Ellen Hedström

SKYHORSE PUBLISHING

Too many cookbooks sit around collecting dust, which is a real shame. Partly because it's a waste of trees and man hours, and partly because many people continue to prepare and eat the same old dishes they have learned to make by heart.

Therefore, we have created this book.

Fifty-two fish and seafood dishes, one for each week of the year. We started with what we love the most apart from food: rock music. The thought of trying to emulate the perfect album in the form of a cookbook seemed bizarre at first, but the more we thought about it, the more it made sense.

Cool cover shots, nice lyrics, the perfect length, and no fillers. Each dish shouldn't take longer to make than it takes to listen to an LP—an excellent goal when cooking—so we have thrown in a few great track tips as well.

Wishing you many pleasant weekends!

Pär-Anders Bergqvist and Anders Engvall

CONTENTS

The number in front of each recipe denotes the week of the year that we think it is most suited for. Obviously you should prepare the dishes when you feel like it, but remember that some ingredients are season specific. Every recipe is designed to serve four people.

DRINK SUGGESTIONS

We have tried to suggest a wide variety of drinks. Each suggestion is designed to show a combination of food and wine that generally works, regardless of the maker or year, even if these have an impact on the perfect combination. We have completely disregarded prices without going overboard.

1. A variety of Oysters.
Fuller's London Porter, England.
An elegant porter, British-style, that just screams tradition and oysters.

2. Bouillabaisse with rouille and garlic croutons.
2009 Palicio de Fefiñanes 1583 Albariño, Rias Baixas, Spain.
Albariño is Spain's premier white wine grape. Here, gently oaked.

3. Northern surf 'n turf with fried fillet of white fish, yellow beetroots, white goats cheese, and dried reindeer meat.
Tenuta dell'Ornellaia La Serre Nuove, Tuscany, Italy.
The Tuscan version of a red Bordeaux with an extra dose of cherries.

4. Garlic fried shrimp with avocado dip and corn chips.
2007 Pares Balta Blanca Cusine Cava, Penedes, Spain.
A fruity Cava that loves garlic.

5. Grilled cusk fish with chimichurri, baked tomatoes, and roasted sweet potatoes.
Nøgne Ø Wit, Det Kompromisslöse Bryggeri (The Uncompromising Brewery), Norway. Fun version of a wheat beer from Norway's coolest micro brewery.

6. Arctic char baked in dill with egg, anchovies, and fennel.
Bärnsten lager, Jämtlands Brewery, Sweden. Old northern Aquavit, Sweden. Northern through and through.

7. Grilled Atlantic halibut with a red wine sauce and Café de Paris butter.
2006 Château Roc de Cambes, Bordeaux, France.
A modern red from Côtes de Bourg that just gets better (and more expensive) with each vintage.

8. Oven-baked trout with roasted cauliflower purée, cucumber salad, and trout roe.

2008 Domaine Aux Moines, Savenniéres, France.
We should all handle the Chenin Blanc grape with exactly this amount of love.

9. Fried monkfish with fennel ragout, roasted peppers, olives, and garlic sauce.
2005 George Breuer Schlossberg Riesling,
Rheingau, Germany.
A large Riesling packed with minerals and mature grapes in droves.

10. Cockles "Bloody Mary-style."
Hoegaarden Wit-Blanche, Belgium.
Classic wheat beer with a smell of bubble bath that handles spicy heat as well as it quenches thirst.

11. Ceviche of haddock with tostones.
NV Tarlant Discobitch, Champagne, France, alternatively 2002 Moet Chandon Vintage, Champagne, France.
Champers with roasted oaky tones and a smidgen extra sugar at the base.

12. Oven-baked cod with fresh beetroots, shrimp, and feta cheese.
2009 Joh Jos Prüm Graacher Himmelreich Riesling
Kabinett, Mosel, Germany.
Perky Riesling with sweetness and acidity in a balance worth striving for.

13. Sole Meunière.
2007 Etienne Sauzet Puligny-Montrachet,
Burgundy, France.
Classic luxury meets classic luxury. A white burgundy with a posh addressee.

14. Fried sea bass with white asparagus, endives, and grapefruit sauce.
2009 Franz Hirtzberger Rotes Tor Grüner Veltliner
Federspiel, Wachau, Austria.
Austria's national treasure, Grüner Veltliner, in the hands of the nation's wine making hero.

15. Poached witch flounder with spinach, morel sauce, and spring onions.
2008 Domaine Fèvre Chablis Premier Cru
Fourchaume, Burgundy, France.
Young Chablis rich in minerals with a sophisticated acidity that it wears well.

16. Brandade with peperonata and roasted garlic.
1993 Viña Tondonia Reserva Blanco, Rioja, Spain.
Traditional white rioja is almost as forgotten as a well-prepared brandade.

17. Deep fried smelt with mojo rojo and potato with blackened leek.
2010 Castello di Ama Rosato, Tuscany, Italy.
Italy's most talented rosé found on a dinner table.

18. Clam chowder with roasted corn.
2009 Radio Coteau La Neblina Pinot Noir, Sonoma Coast, USA.
Californian pinot noir has reached new heights in the hands of wine maker Eric Sussman.

19. Fried mackerel with curry romanesco and deep fried onion rings.
Sierra Nevada Pale Ale, USA.
Musky APA (American Pale Ale) with a humble taste of hops.

20. Flounder with seasonal greens, lost egg, and chive stock.
2009 Juliusspital Würzberger Stein Silvaner GC Trocken, Franconia, Germany.
Headstrong and aromatic white wine from an area where chubby bottles are a must.

21. Tuna burrito with fresh salsa and black bean dip.
Dugges Brandmästare Andréns Törstsläckare (a bitter beer by Dugges ale and porter brewery), Sweden.

The country's best light beer? The cilantro smelling hops urges you to eat Asian.

22. Sea bass with cooked artichoke, lemon butter, and dandelion salad.
2010 Pieropan Soave Classico, Veneto, Italy. Soave can be really complex as long
as you find a good wine maker. Here you go!

23. Fried ocean perch with fresh spring rolls, mando sauce, and warm pak choi.
Dupont Jus de Pomme Pétillant, Normandy, France.
Medium dry apple cider from one of France's best cider and calvados producers.

24. Whole oven-baked turbot with hollandaise sauce.
NV André Jacquart Blanc des Blancs, Champagne, France.
Delightfully crisp champagne where the smell of the white flowers lasts the whole way home.

25. Clay pot herring.
Spirit of Hven Organic Summerschnapps,
Hven, Sweden.
Bombastic elderflower spirit that evokes
memories of summer.

26. Grilled catfish with BBQ sauce, blue potato salad, and spicy pineapple.
2009 Interkardinal Solaris, Åhus, Sweden. A crispy oak character is the foundation of the best dry wine made from Swedish grapes.

27. Smoked perch with pickled vegetables
and creamy eggs.
Lustau Palo Cortado Península Solera reserve, Jerez, Spain.
To be honest, we drink way too little sherry. Its fresh acidity makes it perfect to have both in and with food.

28. Grilled porgies with eggplant caviar
and Mediterranean vegetables.
2004 Château Malartic-Lagravière Blanc,
Bordeaux, France.
White Bordeaux is almost as underappreciated as it is perfect with grilled vegetables.

29. Paella de marisco.
2008 Dominio De Tares Godello, Bierzo, Spain.
Spain's number two white wine grape, Godello, has a bright future.

30. Fried tuna with spicy cress, shiitake mushrooms, and Nori rolls
2008 Marcel Deiss Engelgarten, Alsace, France.
Crazy Marcel Deiss triumphs by growing different grapes all jumbled up together in the vineyard.

31. Thai curry with catfish and crab.
Guldenberg Ale, Brouwerij De Ranke, Belgium.
Creamy, fine-tuned ale with a well-created Belgian sweetness.

32. Fried salmon with apple, porcini mushroom, and Caesar dressing.
2006 Tissot Arbois Sélection, Jura, France.
When oxidization is a style and is made with the right finesse, sparks will fly.

33. Crayfish party with all the trimmings.
Light lager and homemade aquavit.
Push the boat out instead of trying to make things fancy with medium dry wines. It is, after all, a crayfish party.

34. Gazpacho with pepper muffins and tiger prawns.
2009 Raats Family Chenin Blanc.
South Africa's underdog winemaker makes the best possible Chenin Blanc from underdog grapes.

35. Broiled zander with warm tomato salad, crayfish tails, dill, lemon, and horseradish.
2008 Far Niente Chardonnay, Napa Valley, USA.
Elegant and multifaceted American that most of all wants to be French.

36. Soured herring.
Skebo Country beer, Skebo Brewery, Sweden.
The beer nerd's favorite brewery puts the malt first and makes beer that whispers.

37. Fishmonger toast
Sigtuna Black October, Sweden.
Dark lager in German schwarzbier style with a local "Sigtuna" touch.

38. Crab with mustard sauce, crisp bread,
and creamy cheese.
2007 Egon Muller Scharzhofberger Riesling Spätlese, Mosel, Germany.
The Moselle Valley's master outshines himself for each year that passes, both in quality and price.

39. Shellfish pasta with forest mushrooms
and tarragon.
2009 Valle Reale Vigna di Capestrano, Abruzzo, Italy.
Traditional white Italian with natural yeast and real love.

40. Lobster minute.
2005 Arnaud Ente Meursault, Burgundy, France.
Why make things complicated? Mineral
salt and lemon butter on popcorn, yes please!

41. Whitefish roe with Västerbotten rösti, citrusy red onion, and crème fraiche.
Landsort Lager, Nynäshamn Ång brewery, Sweden.
Swedish lager without any connection to the term "make mine a large one."

42. Pollock fillet piccata with saffron risotto and warm tomato salad.
2005 Cigliuti Barbaresco Serraboella, Piemonte, Italy.
Claudia and Silvia Cigliuti catch the grape nebbiolos fine bouquet perfectly.

43. Broiled scallops with chorizo and pebre.
Jasmine Pearls, Fuding, China.
Tea is a trend in many kitchens. A quality jasmine flower is God's gift to our sense of smell.

44. Lobster spaghetti with funnel chanterelle, squash, and artichoke.
2008 William Fevré Grand Cru Vaudésir Chablis, Burgundy, France.
One of the big ones in Chablis, producing outstanding vintages such as 2008. Outstanding wines with a generous fruitiness and concentration.

45. Fried lemon sole with lemon potatoes and zucchini salad.
2008 Domaine Kiralyudvar Tokaji Furmint
Sec, Tokaji Hegyalja, Hungary.
Hungary's unsung hero of crisp white wines from the tokay grape furmint.

46. Warm salmon with tempura.
Matsukura Junmai Shu Sake, Japan.
Sake comes in many guises. Junmai Shu is one of the better ones without added alcohol.

47. Fried cod with pumpkin purée and shallots in red wine.
2008 Domaine Roger Perrin, Chateauneuf-du-Pape, France.
CndP is usually a perfect wine for BBQs with its sweet and warm fruitiness.

48. Moules frites with aioli.
Brasserie Cantillon Rosé de Gambrinus, Anderlecht, Belgium.
Traditionally a very acidic beer flavored with real raspberries. As far from alcopop as you can get.

49. Crayfish gratin with focaccia bread.
NV Ferrari Brut, Trentino-Alto Adige, Italy.
If you want to drink a good Italian sparkling wine, you often find it in Franciacorta where Ferrari holds court. It has nothing to do with red sports cars.

50. Hake with green lentils, soured red cabbage, and a garlic reduction sauce.
2009 Yann Chave Hermitage Blanc, Rhône valley, France.
An adequately aged and robust wine with a full body and spicy fruitiness.

51. Herring and Atlantic herring.
Homemade spiced schnapps; we suggest lemon peel, caraway, and dill.
Homemade is the new luxury.
Do experiment with oaked spirits such as cognac.

52. Canapés.
Tumbo German Pilsner, Eskilstuna beer culture, Sweden.
Within the world of beer, pilsner is a watered-down concept, but there are exceptions.

1

A variety of oysters

◢ A VARIETY OF OYSTERS

If, like Anders, you think that oysters should be eaten just as they are and that any additions are unnecessary, you can skip this page. If, on the other hand, like Pär-Anders, you think that oysters aren't really that tasty, you should definitely try these variations.

Angels on Horseback
8 oysters
8 slices of bacon
8 drops of Tabasco
2 tbsp breadcrumbs
2 tbsp butter for frying

Open the oysters. Place an oyster on each slice of bacon and a drop of Tabasco on each oyster. Roll the oyster in the bacon slice and cover the bacon in breadcrumbs. Fry in the butter and place the "angels" back into the oyster shell.

Oysters with Tomato, Horseradish, and Dill
8 oysters
1 tomato, seeded and diced
1 inch (2 cm) piece of horseradish, grated
3 sprigs of dill
1 tbsp olive oil
Salt and pepper

Open the oysters. Fry the tomato quickly in the oil and add the horseradish and dill. Add salt and pepper to taste. Serve in the shells with the oysters.

Oysters with Shallots and Sherry
8 oysters
1 shallot, finely chopped
¼ cup (50 ml) sherry vinegar

Mix the onion and vinegar and set aside for at least 15 minutes. Open the oyster and add 1 tbsp of the mix in each oyster.

Thai Oysters

8 oysters
¼ cup (50 ml) fish sauce
1 red chili, finely chopped
1 tbsp cilantro, chopped

Mix the fish sauce, chili, and cilantro. Open the oysters and add 1 tbsp in each oyster.

Rockefeller Oysters

8 oysters
½ shallot, finely chopped
1 tbsp butter
1 handful spinach leaves
¾ cup (150 g) cream
1 tbsp Pernod, or an anise-flavored liqueur
1 egg yolk
Salt and white pepper

Open the oysters and pour the liquid from the oysters into a pan. Add the cream and Pernod and heat briefly. Whisk the egg yolk into the mixture and add salt and pepper to taste. Fry the shallot in butter and add the spinach. Add salt and pepper to taste. Place the spinach in the oyster shell and add the sauce. Place in the top rack in the oven and cook at 435°F (225°C) until golden brown.

Album tip: Thin Lizzy *Nightlife*
This classic from 1974 is nice and relaxed, in the same way you might be when you eat oysters.

Bouillabaisse with rouille
and garlic croutons

BOUILLABAISSE WITH ROUILLE AND GARLIC CROUTONS

If you want to learn how to make a really good fish soup, it's enough to master bouillabaisse. Everything else is a copy, or at least simplified versions that derive from the same base. Learning how to pronounce the word bouillabaisse? Well that is a completely different kettle of fish.

Basic Bouillabaisse Soup
2 yellow onions, finely chopped
1 leek (only the white part), finely chopped
4 garlic cloves, chopped
1 fennel, finely chopped
1 carrot, diced
As much celeriac as carrot
1 chili pepper, chopped
1 sprig parsley
½ cup (100 ml) olive oil
1 tbsp tomato purée
1 tsp (½ gram) saffron
1 bay leaf
6 sprigs wild thyme
1¾ cups (400 ml) white wine
1 orange, juice and zest
3 fresh tomatoes, diced
6⅓ cups (1½ liters) fish stock
Salt and white pepper
Around 2 lbs (800 g) mixture of fish and shellfish

Fry the onion, leek, garlic, fennel, carrot, celeriac, chili, and parsley in the olive oil until soft. Add the herbs and white wine, allowing the liquid to absorb. Add tomatoes, orange, and fish stock and simmer for about 30 minutes. Blend into a smooth mixture and pass through a sieve. Add salt and white pepper to taste. The soup is now ready to enjoy with various types of seafood (allow around 6 oz/175 g per person).

Rouille

1 pimento
2 garlic cloves
1 potato, cooked and peeled
2 egg yolks
1 tsp Dijon mustard
1 tsp tomato purée
½ cup (100 ml) cooking oil
½ cup (100 ml) olive oil
Salt and white pepper

Blend the pimento, garlic, potato, egg yolk, mustard, and tomato purée until smooth. Add a little oil at a time so as not to split the sauce. Add salt and white pepper to taste.

Croutons

3 slices of white bread
¼ cup (50 ml) olive oil
1 garlic clove, pressed
1 tsp parsley, chopped

Cut the edges off the bread and into cubes. Fry the cubes in the olive oil until golden brown on medium heat. Add the garlic and parsley. Place the croutons on some paper to drain the excess fat.

Album tip: Rainbow *On Stage*
This benefits from being played back to front. That is to say, start with the B-side's magnificent version of "Mistreated" and end with "Kill the King" and the medley.

Northern surf 'n turf with fried fillet of white fish,
yellow beetroots, white goat cheese,
and dried reindeer meat

NORTHERN SURF 'N TURF WITH FRIED FILLET OF WHITE FISH, YELLOW BEETROOTS, WHITE GOAT CHEESE, AND DRIED REINDEER MEAT

Land and sea, surf 'n turf; culinary kitsch according to some, the best of both worlds according to others. For those of us who come from northern Sweden, eating reindeer meat with almost everything is the norm, but preferably with a piece of white fish and some cheese.

The Fish
4 cleaned fillets of white fish around
  5½ oz (160 g) each
3 tbsp salt
3 tbsp caster sugar
Roughly crushed white pepper
1 sprig dill
1 tbsp cooking oil

Mix the salt, sugar, white pepper, and dill and rub into the fish. Leave it for 3 hours letting the fish lightly marinate in the mixture. Rinse in cold water and dry the fish with some paper towels. Fry the fish on high heat in a bit of oil to give it a nice color without overcooking it.

Album tip: Refused *The Shape of Punk to Come*
This album was released to acclaim the world over. When it was revealed that it hailed from Umeå, even Sweden took note.

Sides

3 cups (400 g) yellow beetroots
1 cup (100 g) white goat cheese,
    cut into pieces
¼ cup (50 g) dried reindeer meat,
    thinly sliced
2 tbsp roasted almonds
1 bunch Mache salad
Salt

Boil the beetroots until soft in salted water. Peel
and mix with the rest of the ingredients creating
a warm salad. Add the honey dressing on top.

Honey Dressing

2 tbsp liquid honey
1 tbsp white wine vinegar
2 tbsp olive oil
Salt
Crushed black
    pepper

Mix the ingredients together and
add salt and pepper to taste.

Garlic fried shrimp with
avocado dip and corn chips

◀ GARLIC FRIED SHRIMP WITH AVOCADO DIP AND CORN CHIPS

Shrimp with aioli tastes great, but it is also one of the reasons that many never discover all the amazing main dishes that include shrimp. This is a simple but far more interesting variety of the standard Friday night menu.

The Shrimp
2.2 lbs (1 kg) fresh shrimp, peeled but with the head still intact
3 garlic cloves, chopped
1½ cups (100 g) parsley, chopped
½ cup (100 ml) olive oil

Heat the oil in the pan. Add the garlic and fry for 30 seconds. Add the shrimp and turn them, frying for two minutes until lukewarm. Add the chopped parsley.

Avocado Dip
2 ripe avocadoes, diced
1 tomato, seeded and diced
1 red onion, finely chopped
1 green chili, chopped
Juice from 1 lime
1 garlic clove, chopped
1 tbsp olive oil
5 drops Tabasco
Salt and black pepper

Mix together all the ingredients and add salt and pepper to taste.

Corn Chips
1 packet of corn tortillas
Oil for frying
Salt

Cut the tortillas into thin strips. Fry in a deep fryer at 325°F (170°C) until it stops bubbling. Place on some paper towels to absorb the excess oil. Add salt to taste.

Album tip: Blackberry Smoke *Little Piece of Dixie*
We could have suggested something cozy in line with Diana Krall, but then we remembered what Friday nights really feel like. Listen to the lyrics in "Good One Comin' On" and you'll see what we mean.

5

Grilled cusk fish with chimichurri,
baked tomatoes, and roasted sweet potatoes

5 GRILLED CUSK FISH WITH CHIMICHURRI, BAKED TOMATOES, AND ROASTED SWEET POTATOES

Cusk is a mixture of cod and anglerfish in its consistency. Chimichurri is a type of Argentinean pesto, which is a bit more acidic as it contains a lot of vinegar. Make sure the grill is boiling hot! And your beer is ice cold!

4 pieces of cusk fish, around 5½ oz (160 g) per person
1 tbsp oil
Salt and pepper

Rub the fish with oil, salt, and pepper. Grill on high heat, 3 minutes on each side.

Chimichurri
¾ cup (75 ml) olive oil
¾ cup (75 ml) red wine vinegar
3 cups (200 g) parsley, chopped
1½ cups (100 g) oregano, chopped
1 tsp cayenne pepper
1 tsp salt

Mix all the ingredients until they resemble a "pesto style" mixture.

The Tomatoes

4 tomatoes on the vine
1 tbsp olive oil
1 tsp sugar
Salt and pepper

Cut a cross in the bottom of the tomatoes and place in the oven for 5 minutes at 435°F (225°C). The skin is now loose, so pull it up towards the top of the tomato. Add oil, salt, pepper, and sugar to the tomatoes and bake for another 10 minutes.

Roasted Sweet Potatoes

6 sweet potatoes cut into wedges
1 tbsp cooking oil
Salt and pepper

Coat the potatoes in the oil, salt, and pepper. Place in the oven, with the peels down, and roast for 20 minutes at 435°F (225°C) so they get slightly burnt at the edges. If you need more time, or you are after a crispy finish, leave them for a bit longer.

Album tip: Backyard Babies
Stockholm Syndrome
Takes the listener hostage and refuses to let go until it's finished. The song "Friends" also contains guest vocals by Joey Ramone.

Arctic char baked in dill
with egg, anchovies, and fennel

6 ARCTIC CHAR BAKED IN DILL WITH EGG, ANCHOVIES, AND FENNEL

If you are really fussy, you might believe that Arctic char should be cooked over an open fire to the sounds of an acoustic guitar being plucked, but this is a cookbook, which means you can't take a chance with either open fires or strumming skills. Bake it carefully. When the char is "opaque" in the middle, it is perfect.

The Char
4 fillets of Arctic char, or trout
1 bunch dill
¼ cup (50 g) butter
Salt and white pepper

Place the dill on a baking tray with the char on top. Add knobs of butter and season with salt and pepper. Bake in the oven for 15 minutes at 275°F (140°C).

Sides
4 boiled eggs, divided
4 anchovy fillets
1 batch chopped chives
2 inch (5 cm) piece of leek, sliced
⅓ cup (100 g) crème fraiche
1 tsp Dijon mustard

Mix all the ingredients to make a cold salad.

The Fennel
2 fennels
1 sprig thyme
1 pinch dill seeds
3 tbsp butter
½ cup (100 ml) white wine
½ cup (100 ml) water
Salt

Divide the fennel in the middle and cook together with the rest of the ingredients for around 15 minutes.

Potato Purée
1 lb (400 g) potatoes
¼ cup (50 g) butter
¾ cup (200 ml) milk
1 bunch dill, chopped
1 tbsp horseradish, grated
Salt and white pepper

Boil the potatoes until soft and mash them. Heat the milk and butter and add to the potatoes. Blend in the dill and horseradish and add salt and pepper to taste.

Album tip: Eddie Vedder *Into the Wild*
The soundtrack to the movie about a guy who donates
all his belongings to charity and takes off for Alaska—
to live on Arctic char.

Grilled Atlantic halibut with a
red wine sauce and Café de Paris butter

GRILLED ATLANTIC HALIBUT WITH A RED WINE SAUCE AND CAFÉ DE PARIS BUTTER

How do you include some classic meat sides into a seafood cookbook? You choose a meaty fish, of course. The original recipe for the Café de Paris butter contains forty-two ingredients, but it gets a bit difficult with the proportions if you are not planning on making 22 lbs (10 kg) of herby butter. In this variety, we have included the most important. Insanely tasty!

The Atlantic Halibut
4 pieces Atlantic halibut, or any halibut,
   around 6 oz (180 g) per person
1 tsp cooking oil
Salt and pepper

Add some salt, pepper, and a thin layer of oil on the halibut. Grill the fish pieces in a really hot pan, which should give a pretty pattern on the fish. Finish the fish off by baking in the oven for 5–10 minutes at 400°F (200°C).

Red Wine Sauce
1 shallot, peeled and chopped
½ garlic clove
1 sprig thyme
1 tsp cooking oil
2 tsp caster sugar
¾ cup (200ml) red wine
2 tbsp balsamic vinegar
1¼ cup (300ml) meat stock
1 tsp corn flour
Salt and white pepper

Fry the shallot, garlic, and thyme in the oil. Add the sugar and caramelize. Pour the red wine and vinegar into the pan and reduce it until ½ cup (100 ml) remains. Add the meat stock and reduce again until ¾ cup (200 ml) remains. Mix the corn flour in a little water and thicken the sauce. Add salt and pepper to taste and finish off by passing the sauce through a sieve.

Café de Paris Butter

1 cup (200 g) butter, room temperature
1 shallot, finely chopped
1 garlic clove, pressed
2 tsp fresh parsley
2 tsp fresh chives
1 tsp fresh sage
½ tsp tarragon
2 anchovy fillets
1 tsp Dijon mustard
1 tbsp capers
1 tbsp freshly squeezed lemon juice
1 pinch cayenne pepper
1 pinch freshly ground black pepper
1 pinch curry powder
½ tsp paprika
2 tsp cognac

Lightly fry the shallot in some butter without giving it color. Allow to cool. Mix the garlic, parsley, chives, sage, tarragon, anchovies, mustard, and capers in a food processor. Whisk the butter until light and airy with an electric hand mixer and mix the rest of the ingredients into the butter.

Warm Bean Salad

2½ cups (300 g) haricot vert, or French green beans
1 package of bacon
1 red onion
3 tbsp olive oil
1 tbsp white wine vinegar
Salt
Crushed black pepper

Cut the bacon into strips and fry until crispy. Remove any excess fat. Cut the red onion into arches and boil the beans in salted water until soft. Mix together and season with salt and black pepper. Serve warm.

Album tip: Metallica's *Black Album*. A meaty dish needs meaty rock. Music doesn't come richer than this and you don't actually need to listen to "Nothing Else Matters."

Oven-baked trout with roasted cauliflower purée,
cucumber salad, and trout roe

8 OVEN-BAKED TROUT WITH ROASTED CAULIFLOWER PURÉE, CUCUMBER SALAD, AND TROUT ROE

Why would you walk into dangerous rapids, dressed only in a pair of oversized rubber boots, a mosquito net, and a fishing rod that is almost impossible to learn how to use? Any guesses?

The Trout
4 pieces of trout, around 6 oz (180 g) per person
1 tbsp butter
4 sprigs of dill
Salt and pepper

Bake the trout together with the dill on a greased baking tray for 20 minutes at 275°F (140°C).

Cauliflower Purée

½ cauliflower head
1 shallot, finely chopped
1 garlic clove, pressed
1 tbsp cooking oil
1 cup (200 ml) cream
¾ cup (200 ml) milk
1 tsp lemon juice
Salt and white pepper

Cut the cauliflower into small pieces and fry in the oil together with the onion and garlic until golden brown. Add the cream and milk and cook until the cauliflower is soft. Mix the cauliflower into a smooth purée and season with salt, white pepper, and lemon juice.

Cucumber Salad
½ cucumber
4 radishes
2 tbsp butter
Salt and white pepper
1 bunch dill
1 bunch water cress
3.5 oz (100g) trout roe

Peel and deseed the cucumber and cut into pieces, slice the radishes, and warm the vegetables carefully in the butter. Batch the dill into small bouquets and use this as garnish together with the water cress and roe.

Album tip: Imperiet *Blå Himlen Blues* (*Blue Sky Blues*)
There's constant talk of the Swedish band Ebba Grön.
In fifteen years, everyone will realize that this was the peak
of Thåström's artistic career.

Fried monkfish with fennel ragout,
roasted peppers, olives, and garlic sauce

9 FRIED MONKFISH WITH FENNEL RAGOUT, ROASTED PEPPERS, OLIVES, AND GARLIC SAUCE

Monkfish is proof that beauty matters on the inside, as it's hard to find an uglier, but tastier, fish. The price is reflected in its taste, so make sure you have a clear idea of how you want to prepare it. Here is one suggestion.

Monkfish

4 pieces of monkfish,
    around 6 oz (180 g) per
    person
Olive oil
Salt and white pepper

Season the fish and fry on a high heat in the olive oil.

Sides

2 red peppers
1 tbsp olive oil
16–20 kalamata olives
1 pot of fresh basil

Brush the pepper with the olive oil and bake for around 15 minutes in the oven at 425°F (225°C) until the skin darkens. Let the pepper cool in a bowl covered in plastic wrap until the skin loosens. Peel, seed, and cut the pep-

Fennel Ragout

2 fennels
1 small yellow onion
¼ cup (50 ml) olive oil
1 garlic clove
1 tsp (½ g) saffron
1 sprig thyme
1 tsp tomato pure
½ cup (100 ml) white wine
Juice of 1 lemon
Salt and white pepper

Cut the fennel and onion into pieces and fry in the olive oil, while stirring, for 5 minutes. Add the garlic, saffron, thyme, and tomato purée and fry the mixture for a few more minutes. Add the white wine and lemon juice and allow to absorb completely into the vegetables. Season to taste with the salt and pepper.

Garlic Sauce

2 garlic cloves, peeled
2 shallots, peeled and finely chopped
¼ cup (50 ml) olive oil
½ cup (100 ml) white wine
1¼ cups (300 ml) chicken stock
¼ cup (50 g) butter at room temperature
Salt and white pepper

Cut the garlic into thin slices, heat the oil and add the garlic, frying until golden brown. Pay attention as it can burn quickly. Add the shallots and white wine, letting it evaporate. Add the chicken stock and reduce until ⅔–¾ cup (150–200 ml) remains. Mix in the butter and add salt and white pepper to taste.

Album tip: Motörhead *Bomber*
Motörhead's singer Lemmy can, just like the monkfish, hardly be accused of being beautiful, but anyone accusing him of lacking vocal talent is sorely mistaken.

Cockles
"Bloody Mary-style"

10 COCKLES "BLOODY MARY-STYLE"

These cockles don't just work well as a dinner, but are also great as party appetizers or for lunch during a hangover. The dish already has a kick, but if you really want it to hurt, just add five more drops of Tabasco. But be careful. . . . Note that even leftovers should ideally be consumed with a few ice cubes.

2.2 lbs (1 kg) cockles
2¼ cups (500 ml) tomato juice
1 small banana shallot, chopped
1 tbsp tomato puree
3 pinches celery salt
2 tsp Worcestershire sauce
10 drops Tabasco
3 pinches salt
1 pinch ground black pepper
2 tbsp olive oil
2 tbsp (30 ml) vodka
3 celery stalks

Fry the onion in the olive oil and add tomato juice, celery salt, Worcestershire sauce, Tabasco, salt, and pepper and bring to the boil. Add the cockles and a lid and boil for 3 minutes. Remove the cockles and add the vodka to the soup. Pour the stock over the cockles and top with the celery.

4 large slices of ciabatta
½ cup (100 ml) olive oil
15 basil leaves
3 sprigs parsley
1 pinch salt

Heat a pan on the stove. Mix the oil, herbs, and salt and coat the ciabatta with the mix. Place in the pan and lightly fry the bread to give it some color.

Tip: Place the cockles in 4 quarts (4 liters) of ice cold water with 1 tbsp of salt. Leave for 45 minutes. (This gets rid of any sand that might have remained in the cockles.)

Album tip: AC/DC *If You Want Blood . . . You've Got It*
Any comments would be superfluous.

Haddock ceviche with tostones

⨼⨼ HADDOCK CEVICHE WITH TOSTONES

We know, ceviche with tostones sounds terribly posh, but it really isn't that difficult to prepare. However, you don't need to tell your wide-eyed dinner guests that.

Ceviche
1.3 lbs (600 g) haddock, diced
The zest and juice of two limes
2 mangoes, diced
2 passion fruits, diced
2 garlic cloves, chopped
1 green chili, chopped
1 red chili, chopped
3 tomatoes, deseeded and diced
3 tbsp olive oil
Salt and black pepper

Mix the haddock and lime and let it marinate for 1 hour. Add the rest of the ingredients and season to taste.

Tostones
2 plantains
1 tsp cinnamon
1 tsp cayenne pepper
1 tsp sugar
1 tsp salt
Oil for frying

Peel the plantains and cut into 1-inch (3 cm) pieces. Mix the dry spices together. Deep fry the banana pieces for about 4 minutes at 300°F (150°C) until soft. Remove and flatten into a patty shape. Fry a second time, but increase the heat to 325°F (170°C). Sprinkle the spice mixture over the bananas and serve immediately.

Album tip: Bad Religion *Against the Grain*
We just felt that some punk rock in the kitchen makes it even more fun to both prepare and serve this dish, and it's not any old punk record either.

Oven-baked cod with fresh
beetroots, shrimp, and feta cheese

OVEN-BAKED COD WITH FRESH BEETROOTS, SHRIMP, AND FETA CHEESE

The combination of fresh beetroot and feta cheese is so incredibly tasty, and with some cod and shrimp it becomes pure magic. It's really one of the best dishes you can eat. Riesling wine, anyone?

Cod

4 pieces of cod, choose the shoulder steak, approx 6 oz (180g) per person
2 tbsp (30 g) salt

Dissolve the salt in 1 quart (1 liter) of water and place the fish in it. Leave it for 1 hour so it becomes lightly pickled and gets a firm consistency. Bake the cod in the oven on a greased baking tray for 15 minutes at 325°F (170°C).

Sides

3 cups (400 g) fresh beetroots
¾ cup (150 g) peeled shrimp
¾ cup (100 g) feta cheese cut into rough chunks
1 bunch chervil
½ cup (50 g) hazel nuts

Roast the hazelnuts in the oven at 435°F (225°C) for 5 minutes before peeling and chopping them. Boil the beetroots in salted water until soft and peel and chop into wedges. Place on plates together with the rest of the ingredients and pour over the vinaigrette.

Shallot and Chervil Vinaigrette

3 shallots
½ cup (100 ml) white wine vinegar
4 tbsp cooking oil
1 tsp chopped chervil
Salt and white pepper

Finely chop the shallots and cook in the white wine vinegar until most of it evaporates. Season with salt and pepper. Let the shallots cool and then add the oil and chopped chervil.

Album tip: Faces "*A Nod Is as Good as a Wink . . .*"
An incredibly good record from start to finish and a reminder that Rod Stewart and Ron Wood were once the coolest dudes in the world.

Sole Meunière

SOLE MEUNIERE

The world's tastiest fish—in all categories. If you haven't eaten sole, you haven't experienced eating real fish. Meunière means "female miller" in French and basically means letting your wife flour the fish before you make it . . . kind of.

4 soles, approx 1 lb (450 g) per person, skinned
2 cups (200 g) flour
1⅓ cups (300 g) butter
1½ cups (100 g) parsley, chopped
2 lemons
1 cup (100 g) horseradish, grated
Salt and pepper

Season the fish first and then coat them in flour. Shake off any excess flour and fry the fish in the butter on medium heat. Fry the fish for 5 minutes on each side. Make sure you keep basting the fish in butter to give it a golden brown color and a lot of love. Add the parsley and coat with some of the butter. Lemon, fried butter, grated horseradish, and boiled potatoes can accompany this dish.

Tip: A sole should preferably have been dead for a while, generally 6–7 days, to tenderize the flesh.

Album tip: Rush *2112*
The title track on the A-side is 20 minutes of pure magic—just enough time to make this dish.

Fried sea bass
with white asparagus, endive,
and grapefruit sauce

FRIED SEA BASS WITH WHITE ASPARAGUS, ENDIVE, AND GRAPEFRUIT SAUCE

Reminiscent in taste and consistency of sole, but that is where the similarities end.

Fish and Asparagus
3 fillets of sea bass
12 white asparagus
1 pinch granulated sugar
4 tbsp cooking oil
Salt and white pepper

Peel the asparagus and boil in salted water for 2 minutes before chilling in cold water. Season the fish fillets with salt and pepper and fry in 2 tbsp cooking oil at a high heat so that the fish get a nice color without being overcooked. Fry the asparagus until golden brown in the rest of the oil and season with salt, pepper, and finish off with a bit of sugar.

Endives
2 endives
2 tbsp cooking oil
2 tbsp sugar
½ cup (100 ml) white wine
2 grapefruits
3 tbsp butter
Fresh herbs
Salt and pepper

Rip out the endives' leaves, cut out wedges of pulp from one grapefruit, and squeeze out juice from the remaining grapefruit. Fry the endive leaves in oil on high heat, add the sugar, and let it caramelize. Pour in the white wine and grapefruit juice and reduce until half the liquid remains. Add small dollops of butter while stirring, and season with salt and pepper. Garnish the dish with the grapefruit wedges and fresh herbs.

Album tip: Smashing Pumpkins *Mellon Collie and the Infinite Sadness*
"Bullet with Butterfly Wings" sounds pretty dangerous too. Okay, that was

15

Poached witch flounder with
spinach, morel sauce, and spring onion

15 POACHED WITCH FLOUNDER WITH SPINACH, MOREL SAUCE, AND SPRING ONION

Fish, potato, vegetables, and sauce, nothing complicated, just incredibly tasty! Since Witch flounder doesn't have the firmest consistency, it easily breaks apart at high heats. Poaching is by far the best way to prepare this fish.

4 fillets of witch flounder, approx 6 oz (180g) per person
1 shallot, chopped
½ cup (100 ml) white wine
¾ cup (200 ml) water
Salt and white pepper

Fold the fillets and place them on a greased baking tray together with the onion, wine, water, and salt and pepper. Bake the fish in the oven for 25 minutes at 260°F (125°C).

Sides

3 cups (100 g) fresh baby spinach
8 spring onions
2 tbsp butter
1½ cups (100 g) morel, fresh or canned
1 shallot, chopped
2 cups (400 ml) cream
1.3 lbs (600 g) fresh potatoes, peeled
Sprigs of dill
Salt and white pepper

Boil the potatoes with salt and a few sprigs of dill. Fry the morels and shallot in half the butter. Add the cream and let the sauce simmer for a few minutes. Season with salt and white pepper. Cut the spring onion into 1-inch (3 cm) pieces and fry together with the spinach in the remaining butter.

Album tip: Monster Magnet *Powertrip*
You can't suggest fifty-two records without including this rock legend. Space Lord!

16

Brandade with peperonata
and roasted garlic

16 BRANDADE WITH PEPERONATA AND ROASTED GARLIC

When the French were making lobscouse they accidently ran out of the salty bit so instead they took dried cod and made a real success of it. The resulting dish was called brandade, which is easier to make than it seems. Just make sure you remove the salt from the fish by soaking it in water 24 hours prior to cooking.

Approx 2 lbs (800 g) potatoes, peeled
7 oz (200 g) salted ling, soaked for 24 hours
¼ cup (50 ml) olive oil
1 garlic clove, chopped
¾ cup (200 ml) milk
Salt and white pepper

Boil the potatoes until soft. Meanwhile, fry the garlic in the olive oil, add the milk, and bring to a boil. Add the ling and simmer for 5 minutes. Remove the fish, peel off the skin, and take out bones. Mash the potatoes and mix in a little of the milk mixture until you have a smooth purée. Add the cooked and now crumbled fish and mix everything together.

Peperonata
1 red pepper, diced
1 yellow pepper, diced
1 red onion, roughly chopped
2 garlic cloves, sliced
3 tbsp olive oil
1 tbsp lemon juice
10 black olives, pitted and quartered
1 tbsp flat leaf parsley, shredded
Salt and pepper

Place the peppers, red onions, garlic, and olive oil in a small pan. Let it simmer for 15 minutes on low heat. Add lemon juice, olives, parsley, salt, and pepper.

Roasted Garlic
1 garlic, divided into cloves
1 tbsp oil

Coat the cloves in oil and roast in the oven at 435°F (225°C) for 10 minutes.

Album tip: Plastic Bertrand *An 1*
A punk classic from 1978 that contains one hit: "Ça Plane Pour Moi." On the other hand, the track is so good that you can play it on repeat at least 10 times.

Deep fried smelt with mojo
rojo and potato with charred leek

18 DEEP FRIED SMELT WITH MOJO ROJO AND POTATO WITH CHARRED LEEK

The smelt is often dismissed as a cucumber-smelling fish of poor quality. In central Europe, however, it has long been known how good this relative of the salmon really is. This variety is similar to the English fish and chips.

1.5 lbs (700 g) small fresh smelts
1¼ cups (150 g) flour
2 tsp salt
Oil for frying

Turn the deep fryer on to 350°F (180°C). Mix oil and salt
and coat the fish. Fry for around 4 minutes, or until
golden brown.

Deep Fried Parsley
1 bunch parsley
Salt

Deep fry the parsley for 30 seconds and dab with paper
towels to absorb excess fat before adding salt.

Mojo Rojo
1 red pepper, roasted and peeled
2 garlic cloves
2 tbsp white wine vinegar
1 slice white bread, cubed
1 egg yolk
2 tsp cumin
2 tsp ground paprika
1 pinch cayenne pepper
2 pinches salt
1½ cup (150 ml) olive oil

Mix all the ingredients in a food
processor, omitting the oil. Then
add the oil little by little
and refrigerate.

Potatoes
½ of a leek
2.2 lbs (1 kg) fresh Cyprus potatoes (or small potatoes
    with thick skin)
1 quart (1 liter) water
¼ cup (100 g) coarse salt

Turn the oven to 480°F (250°C). Tear apart the leek and
bake all the parts in the oven until dry and darkened.
Grind the charred leek to a black powder. Carefully wash
the potatoes and boil in salted water until soft. Take them
out and roll the potatoes in the leek powder to coat.

Tip: The smelt does not need to be gutted
and can be deep fried or fried as is.

Album tip: Mötley Crüe *Too Fast for Love*
Cool and (for its time) innovative. Discover
Los Angeles's finest.

18

Clam chowder with roasted corn

Clam chowder is a stew that was once seen as a poor man's dish. Today's clam chowders should be regarded as creamy soups and are served in every fish and seafood restaurant with pride. Enjoy!

Clams
½ shallot, chopped
1 tbsp olive oil
2.2 lbs (1 kg) clams
¾ cups (400 ml) white wine

Fry the onion with the oil in a pan. Add the clams and wine and cook for 3 minutes. Remove the clams from their shell and save the stock.

The Corn
1 fresh corn on the cob
1 tbsp olive oil
Salt and pepper

Cut out the corn from the cob and mix with the oil. Heat a pan and roast the corn until golden brown. Season to taste.

The Chowder
1 lb (400 g) potatoes, peeled and diced
1 yellow onion, chopped
1 garlic clove, chopped
1 tbsp olive oil
¾ cups (400 ml) stock from the clams
¼ cup (200 ml) milk
1½ cups (300 ml) cream
½ cup (100 ml) water
½ cup (100 g) bacon
Salt and pepper to taste

Fry half the potatoes with the onion and garlic in oil. Add the stock, milk, and cream and cook for 10 minutes. Blend the soup with a handheld mixer. Add the rest of the potatoes and cook for 10 more minutes. Fry the bacon and add it along with corn and clams (the meat only).

Album tip: New York Dolls *Rock 'n' Roll*
New York Dolls were once seen as a poor
man's Rolling Stones. That may be so, but
the record title delivers exactly what it
promises.

19

Fried mackerel with curry romanesco
and deep fried onion rings

19 FRIED MACKEREL WITH CURRY ROMANESCO AND DEEP FRIED ONION RINGS

Album tip: In Flames *A Sense of Purpose*
Swedish metal that has softened with the years, but improved
in quality. This is what American rock would like to sound like,
but however much they try . . . tough luck!

This fish can be thought of as the pride of the Swedish west coast. Here it accompanies our own variant of the west coast salad and onion rings. This is what it would look like if mackerel was served in fast food outlets. Delish!

Mackerel
4 fillets of mackerel
1 tsp cooking oil
Salt and pepper

Season the fillets and fry on a high heat for about 1 minute on each side.

Curry-Roasted Romanesco
½ romanesco broccoli
2 tbsp butter
1 tbsp curry
Salt and white pepper

Divide the romanesco into florets and fry in the butter and curry. Season with salt and pepper.

Deep Fried Onion Rings
2 yellow onions
Corn starch
Oil for frying
Salt

Peel and slice the onion into thin slices. Coat in the corn starch, removing any excess. Deep fry on low heat until the rings are golden brown. Remove the onion and absorb any excess fat with paper towels. Salt to taste.

Green Asparagus
12 green asparagus

Peel and boil the asparagus in salted water for 3–4 minutes.

Crab Salad
1 leg of king crab or a 5 oz (150 g) tin of crab meat
1 granny smith apple
4 tbsp mayonnaise
1 tsp chives, chopped
Salt and crushed black pepper

Peel and cut the crab meat into pieces. Peel the apple and cut into strips. Mix the crab, apple, mayonnaise, and chives and season with the salt and pepper.

Flounder with seasonal greens, lost egg,
and chive stock

20 FLOUNDER WITH SEASONAL GREENS, LOST EGG, AND CHIVE STOCK

If you dropped an egg on the floor in the old days, you probably thought it lost, that is until someone scooped it up and cooked it in some boiling water. Then maybe they added some wine, spices, and some flounder, as well, and discovered that it tasted fantastic.

Flounder

1.5 lbs (700 g) fillet of flounder, 4 pieces at 6 oz
   (175 g) each
1¼ cups (300 ml) water
¾ cup (200 ml) white wine
1 bay leaf
3 white pepper corns
1 tsp salt
¼ cup (50 g) butter
1 bunch chives
Salt and pepper

Boil the water, wine, and herbs and add the fish fillets, simmering for 4 minutes. Remove the fish and add the butter and chives to the stock. Blend with a handheld mixer and season to taste.

Seasonal Greens

8 white asparagus, peeled
16 bunched carrots, peeled
16 green asparagus, peeled
20 sugar snap peas
8 radishes
2 tbsp sugar
3 tsp salt
1 tbsp butter
2 quarts (2 liters) water

Boil water, salt, sugar, and butter and add the white asparagus and carrots. Boil for around 3 minutes and then add the green asparagus and radishes. Boil for a further 3 minutes. Finish off by adding the sugar snap peas and boil for 2 minutes. Remove everything at the same time.

Poached Eggs

4 eggs
2 quarts (2 liters) water
¼ cup (50 ml) white vinegar

Bring water and vinegar to a simmer in a large pan. Break the eggs and let them slowly slide down into the water. Simmer for 3–4 minutes, remove and serve.

Album tip: The White Stripes *Elephant*
What do you do if you lose a band member? You keep going as if nothing happened. Two people, a guitar, and a drum set are all you need to create rock history.

Tuna burrito with fresh
salsa and black bean dip

91 TUNA BURRITO WITH FRESH SALSA AND BLACK BEAN DIP

The difference between a wrap and a burrito is that a wrap is open while a burrito is fastened at the edges. It is therefore vital that you roll the burrito in plastic wrap before preparing it, otherwise you get a tortilla with a sort of tuna hash instead. If prepared correctly, this dish is awesome.

Black Bean Dip

1¼ cups (300 g) black beans, cooked
1 garlic clove, chopped
¼ cup (50 ml) olive oil
1 tbsp caramel color
2 pinches coriander seeds, ground
1 tsp cumin
1 pinch cayenne pepper
2 pinches salt

Dry the beans with a paper towel
to remove any liquid and mix
together all the ingredients.

Salsa

2 tomatoes, seeded and diced
1 papaya, around 1½ cups (300 g), diced
1 red onion, chopped
Juice and zest of 1 lemon
1 tbsp fresh cilantro, chopped
1 green chili, seeded and chopped
1 pinch salt

Mix together all of the ingredients.

Tuna Burritos

8 wheat tortillas, around 8 inches (20 cm) in diameter
1.5 lbs (700 g) fresh tuna, chopped into ½-inch (1
cm) pieces
½ cup (50 g) fresh cilantro, chopped
2 tsp wasabi
1½ tsp salt
1 egg yolk
Oil for deep frying or frying

Mix tuna, wasabi, cilantro, and salt.
Divide the mixture into 8 and roll
into 7-inch-long (18 cm) pieces.
Tightly roll the tuna into the tortillas and
brush the edges with the egg yolk. Roll the
burrito in plastic wrap and seal the edges.
Chill for at least 1 hour before frying.
Deep fry for 5 minutes at 350°F (180°C).

Album tip: Santana *Supernatural*
Not as mind blowing as during the '60s,
but more popular with the chicks.

Sea bass with cooked artichoke,
lemon butter, and dandelion salad

22 SEA BASS WITH COOKED ARTICHOKE, LEMON BUTTER, AND DANDELION SALAD

In the '70s, we made dandelion wine, which was probably more fun than flavorsome. However, in a salad, dandelion leaves are awesome. Just make sure you pick the smallest and most delicate leaves as they taste the best. Sea bass is huge in British pubs. Go discover!

4 sea bass fillets
2 tbsp oil for frying
Salt and pepper

Season both sides of the fish. Then, fry the side with the skin for 2 minutes. Quickly turn to the fleshy side and remove.

Artichoke
4 artichokes
1 lemon
2 sprigs wild thyme
2 tbsp salt
4 quarts (4 liters) water

Boil the water, salt, lemon, and thyme. Add the artichokes and let them simmer until some of the middle leaves loosen. Leave the artichokes in the water until ready to serve.

Lemon Butter
1 cup (200 g) butter
Juice and zest of 1 lemon
3 pinches salt
1 pinch white pepper

Mix all the ingredients in a blender until you have a smooth butter.

Dandelion Salad
1 quart (1 liter) small, delicate dandelion leaves
2 slices of white bread, cubed and roasted in the oven
½ red onion, cut into slivers
½ cup (100 g) smoked bacon, fried until crispy then diced
2 tbsp white wine vinegar
¼ cup (50 ml) olive oil
Salt and pepper

Rinse and dry the dandelion leaves thoroughly. Mix all the ingredients and finish off with the roasted croutons.

Album tip: Wolfmother's self-titled debut. In the '70s, you drank dandelion wine and listened to Zeppelin. This is almost the same thing, just a bit more "now."

Fried ocean perch with fresh spring rolls,
mando sauce, and warm pak choi

FRIED OCEAN PERCH WITH FRESH SPRING ROLLS, MANDO SAUCE, AND WARM PAK CHOI

Ocean perch belong to the family of rock fish, or rock cod, and can live as deep as 1,000 yards (900 meters) under the sea surface. It's an underrated fish that works superbly with a variety of Asian Sides. It's messy to gut and clean, so ask your fishmonger to do this for you.

Ocean Perch

4 rose fish fillets, around 5½ oz (160 g) per person, scaled but with the skin still on

1 tbsp oil for frying
Salt and pepper

Fry the fillets on high heat, skin side down, for 3 minutes. Turn quickly and they're done.

Spring Rolls

1 packet of cellophane noodles, boiled and cooled
1 large carrot, finely grated
6 inch (15 cm) piece of leek, finely sliced
3 cups (100 g) alfalfa sprouts
1 red chili, chopped
1 pot fresh cilantro, chopped
¼ cup (50 ml) mando sauce
12 pieces of rice paper, 8½ inches (22 cm)

Mix the noodles, carrot, leek, sprouts, chili, cilantro, and mando sauce. Place the rice paper in luke-warm water for 1 minute or until it can be rolled. Place the rice paper on a damp kitchen towel with a little of the noodle salad on one side. Fold in the edges and roll the paper into a spring roll. Place the rolls on some damp parchment paper until they are ready to serve.

Mando Sauce

½ cup (100 ml) syrup
½ cup (100 ml) light soy sauce
1 tsp sesame oil
1 tsp white vinegar
2 pinches cayenne pepper
2 tbsp sesame seeds, roasted

Mix together all the ingredients.

Pak choi

2 pak choi, split lengthwise
1 tbsp cooking oil
2 tbsp fish sauce

Fry the pak choi on one side in the oil. Turn and add the fish sauce letting it reduce. Done!

Album tip: Nirvana "*Nevermind*" Because it's still one of the best rock albums ever made and because the band's name is so suited for this recipe.

Whole oven-baked turbot
with hollandaise sauce

🎸 WHOLE OVEN-BAKED TURBOT WITH HOLLANDAISE SAUCE

The turbot may not look very exciting (or does it?) but it is really in a class of its own when it comes to taste and consistency. It's as if God had created a large fillet, dressed it in sand paper, and singled it out on the ocean floor. If turbot is not available, you can substitute it with flounder.

The Fish
3–4 lbs (1½–2 kg) turbot, whole (or flounder)
Approx ¼ cup (30 g) butter
Coarse salt

Salt the fish and bake in the oven on a greased baking tray at 210°F (100°C). Allow 1 hour per 2.2 lbs (1 kg) of fish.

Sides
0.9 lb (400 g) fresh potatoes, peeled
12 white asparagus, peeled
4 quail eggs
1¾ cups (100 g)
   chanterelles, fresh
2 tbsp butter
3.5 oz (100 g)
   shrimp, peeled
Mixed fresh herbs
   (e.g. spinach,
   dill, chives)

Boil the potato and asparagus. Boil the quail eggs, take off the peels, and chop the eggs. Fry the chanterelle mushrooms in the butter and mix everything with the shrimp and herbs to make a lovely warm salad.

Hollandaise Sauce
1 cup (200 g) butter
4 egg yolks
2 tbsp water
1–2 tbsp lemon juice
Salt

Melt the butter and let the fat form on top. Skim the fat with a spoon without getting any of the liquid and keep the clarified butter at a temperature of 105–110°F (40–45°C). Whisk the egg yolks with water in a bowl over a water bath (a pot with boiling water). When the egg yolks have thickened to a creamy consistency, remove the bowl. Add the clarified butter a little at a time, constantly stirring. Season to taste with the lemon juice, salt, and cayenne pepper.

Album tip: Guns N' Roses *Appetite for Destruction*
This record doesn't have a thing to do with turbot, but somehow it works. The world's best rock and the world's best fish . . . yeah, you get it.

25

Clay pot herring

25 CLAY POT HERRING

The name derives from the fact that you layer the ingredients in a clay pot. It's absolutely delicious! And perfect for midsummer celebrations. Watch out if you try to make your own pickled herring: Even the professionals have a hard time getting it right. Instead, put your money on "real" pickled herring instead of the cheaper version. There is a reason for the price difference.

4 large fillets of pickled herring (or 8 smaller ones)
8 eggs, hardboiled and chopped
8 potatoes, boiled and warm
1 red onion, finely chopped
2 cups (100 g) chives, finely chopped
1 pot of dill
½ cup (100 g) butter

Turn the oven to 335°F (175°C). Layer the potatoes, herring, red onion, and chives in an ovenproof dish. Fry the butter in a pan. Place the dish in the oven for 10 minutes, sprinkle some dill over it, and finish off with the warm butter.

Album tip: The Beatles *Let It Be*
It doesn't really matter which of the Beatles' records you choose, as they are all so incredibly good. However, this one just happens to contain the track "Get Back."

Grilled catfish with
BBQ sauce, blue potato salad,
and spicy pineapple

26 GRILLED CATFISH WITH BBQ SAUCE, BLUE POTATO SALAD, AND SPICY PINEAPPLE

The texture of catfish is almost the same as that of angler fish but at half the price. In addition, it is perfect for grilling, just make sure the barbeque is really hot. Blue potato salad tastes like normal potato salad but is a bit more "rock and roll," and that, as we know, is half of what cooking is all about.

Catfish
4 pieces of catfish, approx 6 oz (175 g) per
   person
2 garlic cloves, chopped
2 tbsp olive oil
Salt and pepper

BBQ Sauce
2 garlic cloves, chopped
½ cup (100 g) brown sugar
½ cup (100 ml) Japanese soy sauce
½ cup (100 ml) ketchup
1 tsp liquid smoke
Tabasco to taste

Light the grill. Rub the fish with garlic, oil, salt, and pepper. Heat the soy sauce, garlic, and sugar and cook for 5 minutes before adding the rest of the ingredients. Add Tabasco to taste.

Pineapple

½ pineapple, in wedges
1 tsp cinnamon
1 tsp cayenne pepper
1 tsp salt
1 tsp sugar

Mix cinnamon, cayenne pepper, salt, and sugar. Add plenty of the spice mixture to the pineapple wedges. On an incredibly hot grill, throw on the fish and pineapple, bada bing, and you're done!

Potato Salad

1.6 lbs (800 g) Blue Congo potatoes,
   boiled and chilled
1 cup (100 g) spring onion
1 cup (50 g) flat leaf parsley
½ cup (100 g) crème fraiche
1 cup (200 g) natural yogurt, around 8% fat
Salt and pepper

Peel and dice the potatoes. Chop the onion and parsley and mix the rest of the ingredients. Season to taste.

Album tip: Ace Frehley's solo album from 1978.
It has a blue cover! It has the world's coolest rock star on vocals!!
It includes "New York Groove"!!!
And "Rip it Out"!!!!

Smoked perch with pickled
vegetables and creamy egg

SMOKED PERCH WITH PICKLED VEGETABLES AND CREAMY EGG

To fish for perch is one of the meanings of life. To then smoke it is about the tastiest thing you can do with it. Reflect on this when day-to-day life gets you down.

Perch
Approx 1½ cups (150 g) wood chips
8 small perch, scaled and gutted
1 tbsp salt

Pickled Vegetables
½ tsp white vinegar, 12%
½ cup (100 g) granulated sugar
⅔ cup (150 ml) water
½ cucumber, seeded
1 red onion
1 endive

Creamy Egg
2 medium-cooked eggs
1 cup (200 g) crème fraiche
2 tbsp caviar (a cheaper variety is fine)
2 tbsp dill, chopped
Salt and pepper to taste

Light the grill (preferably a round grill) and start boiling some potatoes if you would like it as an accompaniment.

Salt the fish and set aside for 15 minutes. Meanwhile mix together the vinegar, sugar, and water. Julienne the vegetables and add to the vinegar mixture. Chop the eggs into ¼-inch (½ cm) pieces and mix with the rest of the ingredients.

Smoking
Make a 6 x 6 inch (15 x 15 cm) tray by folding some aluminum foil with a 1-inch (3 cm) edge. Add the wood chips and place the tray on the hot coals. Place the grate on top and then the fish. Finally add the lid and wait 15 minutes. Abracadabra and you are done!

Tip: If you haven't yet bought a mandolin for the vegetables, do so now.

Album tip: Kyuss *Sky Valley*
When the sun sets, it is pretty satisfying to
crank up some desert rock and smoke a perch.

28

Grilled porgies with eggplant caviar
and Mediterranean vegetables

28 GRILLED PORGIES WITH EGGPLANT CAVIAR AND MEDITERRANEAN VEGETABLES

2 porgies (or sea bream, it is the same)
2 garlic cloves, chopped
1 tbsp olive oil
2 tbsp flat leaf parsley, chopped
Salt and black pepper

Eggplant Caviar
1 eggplant
1–2 garlic cloves
¼ cup (50 ml) olive oil
1 tbsp lemon juice
1 tbsp parsley, chopped
Salt and black pepper

Grilled Vegetables
1 zucchini
1 red pepper
1 yellow pepper
2 red onions
½ cup (100 ml) olive oil
2 tbsp white balsamic vinegar
1 cup (100 g) arugula
Salt and black pepper

Light the grill. Mix the garlic, olive oil, parsley, salt, and pepper and marinate the fish for 15 minutes. Cut the eggplant lengthwise and place on the grill, skin down. Leave for 10 minutes on the hottest part (it doesn't matter if the skin gets charred). Scoop out the flesh and peel off a fifth of the skin. Mix the flesh and skin and add the rest of the ingredients. Season to taste with salt and pepper and chill. Mix the vegetables with half the oil, salt, and pepper. Place the fish and the vegetables on the grill and leave for 15 minutes. Mix the vegetables with the arugula and vinegar. Season to taste with salt and pepper.

Tip: If you are in a hurry, use charcoal instead of briquettes.

Album tip: The Lords of the New Church *Killer Lords*
If anyone asks what you are listening to, you can answer Lords of the New Church

Paella de marisco

29 PAELLA DE MARISCO

Traditional Spanish food that gets its name after the large pans that you use to make paella. If you don't have the time or inclination to get a real paella pan, you can use that old wok that you got for Christmas in 1990.

The Rice
¼ cup (50 ml) olive oil
1 red pepper, chopped
2 shallots, finely chopped
2 cups (400 g) Arborio rice
1 tsp (½ gram) saffron
1 bay leaf
¾ cup (200 ml) white wine
3 cups (700 ml) chicken stock
2 garlic cloves, chopped
1 chili, chopped
2 tomatoes, peeled, seeded, and chopped
1 cup (100 g) sugar snap peas
12 cherry tomatoes
Salt and white pepper

Shellfish

1 squid tentacle, in 4 pieces
11 oz (300 g) blue mussels, washed
11 oz (300 g) cockles
4 tiger prawns
4 crayfish, raw
4 scallops
7 oz (200 g) shrimp, peeled
1 lobster, cooked
1 bunch fresh, mixed herbs
Lemons
Aioli (see p. 196)

Fry the shallots in the olive oil without giving it any color. Add the rice, pepper, saffron, garlic, chili, bay leaf, and chopped tomatoes. Fry for another 1 minute and add the white wine, letting it reduce. Dilute with the chicken stock and add salt and pepper to taste. Let the risotto simmer for 20–25 minutes and then add the fish. Start with the squid, blue mussels, cockles, tiger prawns, and crayfish. Cook for 5–6 minutes and then add scallops, lobster, prawns, sugar snap peas, and cherry tomatoes and cook for a couple more minutes. Finish of the paella with a garnish of fresh herbs.

Album tip: Electric Boys *Groovus Maximus*
Everyone has heard "All Lips N' Hips" and that track with Svullo, but really it's this album that is the best—it's just that not everyone has discovered it yet.

Fried tuna with spicy cress, shiitake
mushrooms, and nori rolls

50 FRIED TUNA WITH SPICY CRESS, SHIITAKE MUSHROOMS, AND NORI ROLLS

Pickled tuna has tricked the taste buds of many. In its raw form, it is actually something completely different. Tuna is also, because it is so rich in flavor, a very satisfying fish to work with. Here is a Japanese-inspired variety.

Tuna

4 pieces of tuna, approx 6 oz (180 g) per person
Sesame oil
Salt and white pepper

Season the fish and fry at a high heat in the sesame oil (it should still be red in the middle).

Soy Dressing

1¼ cups (300 ml) Kikkoman soy sauce
⅓ cup (75 ml) sesame oil

Boil the soy sauce until ½ cup (100 ml) remains. Pour the sauce into a narrow glass and leave it to cool so the salt sinks to the bottom. Spoon out the soy, leaving the salt and mix with the sesame oil.

Sides

2 cups (100 g) shiitake mushrooms
2 pak choi
2 tbsp roasted sesame seeds
2 tbsp sesame oil

Fry the mushrooms and pak choi in the oil and sprinkle with sesame seeds on top.

Cress Sauce

½ cup (100 g) crème fraiche
2 pots of garden cress
Salt and pepper

Cut the cress and mix together with the crème fraiche. Season with salt and pepper.

Nori Rolls

2 cups (350 g) sushi rice
1¾ cups (400 ml) water
3 tbsp rice vinegar
3 tbsp granulated sugar
½ tsp salt
2 nori sheets
½ cucumber cut into sticks

Rinse the rice in running cold water for 20 minutes. Place the rice in a pan and add 1¾ cups (400 ml) water and bring to the boil. Reduce the heat and simmer for 15 minutes under a lid. Remove the rice from the heat and leave for a further 15 minutes without the lid, but covered with a towel.

Mix vinegar, sugar, and salt and stir until the sugar has melted. Place the rice in a bowl and pour in the vinegar mixture over the rice, stirring with a wooden spoon until the rice has cooled.

Place a nori sheet on a sushi mat and spread a ¼-inch (½ cm) thick layer of rice. Leave a ½-inch (1 cm) edge at one end that will be the end of the roll. Add the cucumber at the other end and roll into a firm roll. Make another roll and then cut them into 8 pieces.

Album tip: Rollins Band *Nice*
This hasn't got a thing to do with Japan but it is nice to cook to.

Thai curry with catfish and crab

THAI CURRY WITH CATFISH AND CRAB

Okay, we might as well say it: Thai curry should be hot. You can then debate whether it should be hot as hell or just make you a bit thirsty. It's trial and error to be honest, but remember—you can always add heat afterwards, the other way around is a bit trickier.

The Curry Base
tbsp cooking oil
stalk lemongrass, crushed
6 kaffir lime leaves
garlic clove, chopped
1–2 tbsp green curry paste (depending on how much heat you are after)
tsp turmeric
1½ tbsp fish sauce
½ tbsp honey
2 cans coconut milk
tbsp lime juice
½ red chili

Fry the lemongrass, lime leaves, garlic, turmeric, and curry paste in the oil. Add the coconut milk and the rest of the ingredients and cook for 10 minutes.

Sides
1.1 lbs (500 g) catfish, cut into pieces
8 crab claws
tbsp cooking oil
cup (100 g) okra, cut down the middle (strange vegetable so can be omitted)
½ zucchini, cut into pieces
carrot, peeled and cut into sticks
bunch cilantro or sweet basil
Salt

Fry the vegetables in the oil. Add the fish and crab claws and salt to taste. Add the curry base and bring to a boil. Finish off with the herbs.

Album tip: Red Hot Chili Peppers *Blood Sugar Sex Magic*
From the era when everything producer Rick Rubin touched turned to gold. The best funk/rock album in the world, no question about it.

Fried salmon with apple, porcini mushroom,
and Caesar dressing

FRIED SALMON WITH APPLE, PORCINI MUSHROOMS, AND CAESAR DRESSING

There are countless ways to prepare salmon. This specific combination with porcini mushroom, Parmesan, and Caesar dressing is popular in Italy, where a lot of porcini mushrooms are eaten. However, we picked this one as it was one of the more autumnal salmon recipes that we could think of. All good stuff.

Salmon
4 pieces of salmon, 6 oz (180 g) per person
Cooking oil
Salt and pepper

Season the fish and fry at a medium heat in the oil.

Sides
3 apples, Granny Smith
3¾ cups (200 g) fresh porcini mushrooms
2 tbsp flat leaf parsley, chopped
2 parsnips
½ cup (50 g) Parmesan, shaved
3 tbsp cooking oil
1 tbsp butter
Salt and white pepper

Peel and cut the parsnips into wedges. Pour 1 tbsp of oil over them and season with the salt and pepper. Oven roast for around 15 minutes at 350°F (180°C). Peel and cut the apples into wedges. Divide the mushrooms into smaller pieces if they are large and then fry until golden brown in the rest of the oil and butter. Add the apple wedges towards the end. Season with salt and white pepper and add the parsley and the Parmesan.

Caesar Dressing
2 egg yolks
1 garlic clove
2 anchovy fillets
2 tbsp Parmesan, grated
1 tsp Dijon mustard
1 tsp crème fraiche
½ cup (100 ml) cooking oil
Lemon juice
Salt and white pepper

Mix egg yolks, garlic, anchovy, Parmesan, mustard, and crème fraiche in a blender. Add the oil a little at a time to avoid the sauce splitting. Season to taste with salt, pepper, and lemon juice.

Album tip: Mother Earth *You Have Been Watching*
Matt Deighton and his electro-rock-funk-collective make it the perfect record to cook to, no more, no less. You can probably dance to it, too.

Crayfish party with all the trimmings

CRAYFISH PARTY WITH ALL THE TRIMMINGS

A traditional Swedish crayfish party is incredibly good fun and this is all you need for the perfect party.

- Crayfish (important not to forget)
- Västerbotten pie
- Kryddost (spiced cheese)
- Butter
- Sliced bread
- A toaster
- Music sheets
- Lots of napkins or paper towels
- An abundance of beer and spirits
- Water
- A pleasant atmosphere

Västerbotten Pie
Crust
2½ cups (300 g) flour
½ tsp salt
½ cup (125 g) cold butter
1 egg

Filling
3 cups (300 g) Västerbotten cheese, grated
½ cup (100 ml) cream
¾ cup (200 ml) milk
4 egg yolks
1 egg
1 pinch salt
1 pinch pepper

Mix all the ingredients together, either with your fingertips or in a food processor. Flatten the dough into a pie dish with a 10-inch (25 cm) diameter and refrigerate for 30 minutes. Blind bake the pie crust at 400°F (200°C) for 12 minutes. Mix the ingredients for the filling and pour into the crust. Bake for another 30 minutes at the same temperature.

Welcome Drink and Appetizer
Approx 1.5 x 1.5 fl. oz
 (40 x 40 ml) Aquavit in a
 schnapps glass
4 large dill flavored chips

Ulla's Mix
3.5 oz (100 g) smoked common
 whitefish (Lavaret), gutted
½ yellow onion, chopped
1 hardboiled egg, minced
10 straws of chive
3 sprigs dill
3 tbsp mayonnaise
1½ cups (100 ml) cream, whipped
Salt and pepper

Mix all of the ingredients and place on top of the chips. Whatever
is left will be consumed around midnight, guaranteed.

Cooking the Crayfish
4.4 lbs (2 kg) live crayfish
3 quarts (3 liters) water
½ cup (150 g) coarse salt
1 tbsp dill seeds
Crown dill, 15 crowns

Boil the water, salt, and dill
seeds. Add half the dill crowns
and boil together for 5 minutes,
then remove the dill crowns. Place
the crayfish in the boiling stock and
add the rest of the dill crowns. Boil
the crayfish for 4 minutes then chill
as quickly as possible by placing the
pan in a cold water bath. Wait at least
24 hours before eating.

Tip: Place the crayfish in cold water in
a large pot to rinse them slowly over a
few hours. This way you get rid of muddy
remnants and fishy taste.

Album tip: At crayfish parties you do your
own singing.

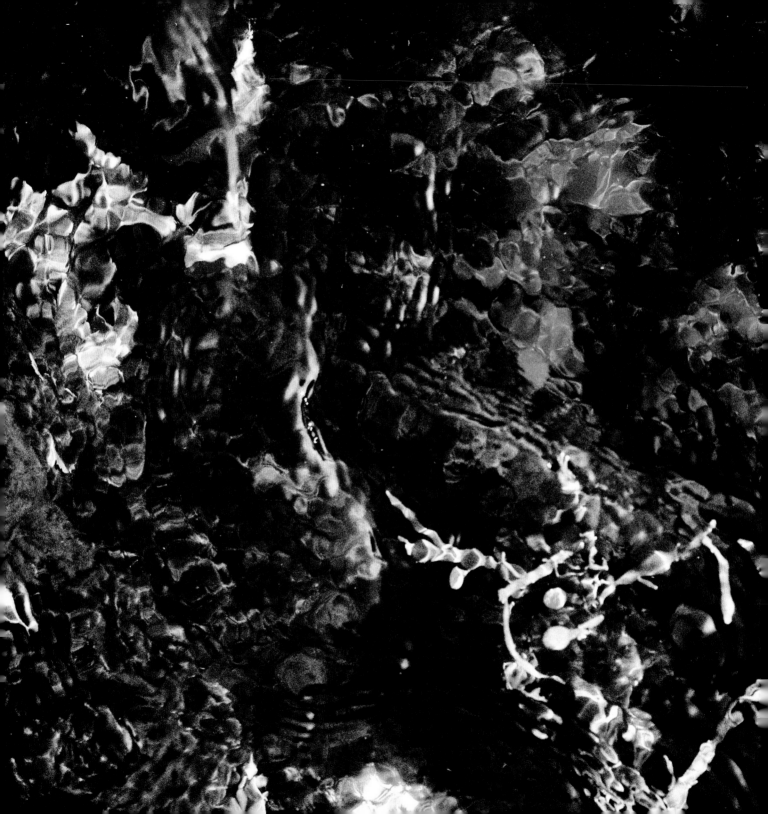

Gazpacho with pepper muffins
and tiger prawns

GAZPACHO WITH PEPPER MUFFINS AND TIGER PRAWNS

If we could choose a dish to take to a desert island, we have come to the conclusion that gazpacho and pepper muffins are top of the list. We would catch and grill the tiger prawns ourselves. Still not sure where we would get the ice from though.

Gazpacho
1 garlic clove
¼ cup (50 ml) olive oil
1.1 lbs (½ kg) tomatoes, diced
1 red pepper, seeded and diced
1 cucumber, roughly grated
1 red onion, peeled and diced
1 chicken stock cube, dissolved in 1¼ cups (300 ml) water
1 red Spanish pepper
2 tbsp tomato purée
2 tbsp white wine vinegar
1 cup (200 g) ice, to serve
¾ cup (200 ml) rapeseed oil
¼ cup (50 g) black olives, pitted and chopped
2 cups (200 g) Manchego cheese, grated
2 tbsp parsley, chopped
Salt and black pepper

Place all the vegetables, except the cucumber, in a mixer to form a smooth soup. Add the rest of the ingredients and cool with ice when ready to serve.

Prawns
32 tiger prawns, peeled
½ cup (100 ml) olive oil
2 garlic cloves, chopped
Salt and pepper

Place the prawns on skewers, marinate, and grill

Pepper and Olive Muffins, Makes 12

4 cups (500 g) Manitoba flour (or a strong wheat
flour with a high protein count)
¾ cup (100 g) porridge oats
1 Spanish pepper, deseeded and chopped
2 tsp baking powder
1 tsp salt
1 tsp black pepper
2 eggs
1 cup (250 ml) milk
½ cup (100 ml) rapeseed oil
¼ cup (50 g) black olives, pitted and chopped
2 cups (200 g) Manchego cheese, grated
2 tbsp parsley, chopped

Mix all the dry ingredients together. Mix the eggs, milk, oil,
olives, cheese, parsley, and Spanish pepper. Blend the dry
ingredients into the wet. Divide the batter between the
muffin cups and bake in the center of the oven for
20 minutes at 400°F (200°C).

Album tip: Deep Purple *In Rock*
If you have this album, you really
need nothing else. Well that was
the original plan. Then we started thinking about *Stormbringer*
and then we took a drink.

Broiled walleye with warm tomato salad,
crayfish tails, dill, lemon, and horseradish

55 BROILED WALLEYE WITH WARM TOMATO SALAD, CRAYFISH TAILS, DILL, LEMON, AND HORSERADISH

It's a bit odd fishing walleye, as it doesn't flap but rather tries to make itself as heavy as possible. When you get them out of the water, they just lie there and stare at you with their strange cat eyes.

4 fillets of walleye, scaled
2 tbsp rapeseed oil for frying
1 lemon
8 tomatoes on the vine
2 red onions
3.5 oz (100 g) crayfish tails
½ cup (100 g) olive oil
2 inch (5 cm) piece of horseradish
½ cup (50 g) dill

Coarsely chop the tomatoes and red onion. Wash and grate the zest of the lemon peel. Squeeze out the lemon and mix the juice, zest, and olive oil in a pan. Broil the zander on very high heat for 2 minutes, skin down, and then another minute on the flesh side. Warm the lemon and oil and add the red onion, letting it simmer for 1 minute. Add the rest of the ingredients and serve.

Album tip: Judas Priest *Screaming for Vengeance*
Simply because the song "Electric Eye" is so befitting
of the Zander; but it's also one of the best albums
in the world.

Soured herring

56 SOURED HERRING

Those of you who eat soured herring already know what to do. Here is
an alternative for you weaklings who opt for hotdogs instead.

The Herrings
16 fresh herrings
⅓ cup (100 ml) sour cream
2 cups (200 g) rye flour
2 tbsp butter for frying
Salt and white pepper

Turn the herring in the sour cream and then coat in the rye flour. Fry in
the butter until golden brown and season to taste.

Sides

1 lb (400 g) potatoes
1 red onion, sliced into
   arches
12 cherry tomatoes
1 bunch dill, chopped
3¾ cups (200 g)
   chanterelles
1¼ cups (300 ml) cream
3 tbsp white vinegar
2 tbsp butter
1 bunch chives, chopped
3.5 oz (100 g) white fish roe
Bunches of dill
Salt and white pepper

Boil the potatoes until soft, leaving the skin on. Peel the potatoes and slice (the potato should be warm when served). Mix together the cream and vinegar and blend together with the potatoes, onion, tomatoes, and dill. Season with the salt and pepper. Fry the mushrooms in the butter and add salt, pepper, and a sprinkle of chives. Garnish with the roe, some dill, and serve with freshly baked Swedish flat bread.

Album tip: Black Crowes *Shake Your Moneymaker*
This is so entrancing that your neighbors won't even realize you're making these pungent herrings.

Fishmonger toast

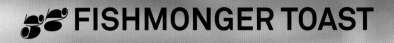 FISHMONGER TOAST

Saturday morning, 9:15 AM. It doesn't get better than this!

4 slices of bread for toasting
12 eggs
⅔ cups (150 g) butter
1 bunch chives, chopped
1 lb (400 g) trout roe
Salt and pepper

Fry the bread in some of the butter. Boil the eggs for 3 minutes, peel and
mash with a fork while still warm. Add the rest of the butter into the egg
mixture and stir the egg mixture in a pan on the stove. Add salt and pepper
and gently stir in the chives. Place the scrambled eggs on the bread and
finish off with a generous amount of trout roe.

Album tip: Slash's solo album
Name an album that you haven't listened to while eating
a roe sandwich. Right now this one fits the bill, especially
the tracks with Myles Kennedy on vocals.

Crab with mustard sauce,
crisp bread, and creamy cheese

58 CRAB WITH MUSTARD SAUCE, CRISP BREAD, AND CREAMY CHEESE

If you are able to purchase ready-cooked crab from the store, then do. Ask them to divide the crab for you to ensure it is well-packed. It should not contain empty space, nor should it be too runny. If you are only able to buy vacuum-packed crab, you can use the recipe below to re-cook it.

Re-cooking Crab
4 crabs, 1.1 lbs (500 g) each
3 quarts (3 liters) of water
⅓ cup (100 g) salt
1 tbsp dill seeds

Boil salt, water, and dill seeds. Remove the crab from the plastic and pour the boiling stock over it. Let the crab cool in the stock, and for best results, leave it until the following day.

Creamy Cheese
1 cup (100 g) grated kryddost, or a
  spiced cheese
1 cup (100 g) grated cheddar cheese
¼ cup (50 g) butter
1 tsp caraway
2 tbsp whisky
1 pinch black pepper

Blend all the ingredients in a food processor and leave overnight.

Mustard Sauce
3 tbsp Swedish mustard, or regular mustard
1 tbsp white wine vinegar
2 tbsp granulated sugar
½ cup (100 ml) cooking oil
1 pinch white pepper
2 tbsp dill, chopped
2 tsp mustard seeds
1 tbsp horseradish, grated

Mix mustard, vinegar, and sugar. Add the oil drop by drop while stirring and mix in the rest of the ingredients.

Album tip: Prodigy *The Fat of the Land*
This record has a crab on the front cover. It
includes the track that must not be named

Crisp Bread

¾ cup (200 ml) lukewarm milk
1 tsp sugar
1 tbsp (15 g) yeast
2 cups (200 g) coarse rye flour
2½ cups (300 g) Manitoba flour
 (or a strong wheat flour with
 a high protein count)
2 tsp coarse salt
2 tbsp dill, finely chopped
Flour for kneading

Mix the milk, yeast, and sugar. Add the flour and mix in a food processor using the dough hook attachment for around 4 minutes. Place in the fridge for one hour. Place on a floured surface and divide the dough in two, rolling each piece thinly, to around a tenth of an inch (3 mm) thickness. Brush the dough with some water, sprinkle the dill on top, and use a rolling pin to integrate it with the dough. Cut the dough into 1 inch-wide (2 cm) sticks. Set aside for 30 minutes and then bake for 7 minutes at 435°F (225°C). If they stuck together while baking, cut with a knife to separate. To make them really crispy, allow them to dry overnight in the oven.

39

Shellfish pasta with
forest mushrooms and tarragon

59 SHELLFISH PASTA WITH FOREST MUSHROOMS AND TARRAGON

Very few really know how good fried crayfish tails are; everyone else will find out with this dish. Most people have eaten tiger prawns, but even if the shells look good, make sure you peel them first. To cook tiger prawns with the shell on just proves how lazy the chef is.

4 raw crayfish tails, peeled
8 scallops
16 tiger prawns
2 tbsp rapeseed oil
Salt and paper

1.1 lbs (500 g) spaghetti or tagliatelle pasta
2¼ cups (150 g) fresh forest mushrooms
    such as penny bun, chanterelle, or black trumpet
2 tbsp butter
1 tbsp flat leaf parsley, shredded
¾ cup (200 ml) milk
1 cup (200 ml) cream
2 tbsp corn starch
1 tsp (5 g) fresh tarragon
1 cup (100 g) Parmesan,
    grated
Salt and pepper

Cook the milk and cream and thicken with the corn starch. Add salt and pepper to taste. Boil the water for the pasta. Cut the mushroom into medium-sized pieces and fry in the butter. Heat a frying pan and fry the shellfish in the oil. Boil the pasta. Add the tarragon and Parmesan to the sauce and the parsley to the mushrooms. Mix the pasta in the sauce and season to taste. Add the rest of the ingredients and serve.

Album tip: The Hives *Tyrannosaurus Hives*
Of course there are lots of bands that are more famous than The Hives. The question is, are there any cooler ones? We don't think so.

Lobster minute

🐟 LOBSTER MINUTE

Not a lot compares to freshly-cooked lobster with butter and grated horseradish. In addition, sitting on the bus with four live lobsters in a bag is a very cool feeling. But watch out, these fellows won't hesitate to pinch off your finger if given the chance.

4 live lobsters, around 1 lb each (500 g)
⅓ cup (100 g) salt for each 3 quarts
(3 liters) of water
1 tbsp dill seeds for each 3 quarts
(3 liters) of water
½ cup (100 g) clarified butter
2 inch (5 cm) piece of horseradish,
grated
2 lemons
1 pot of dill

In two pots, boil 3 quarts (3 liters) of water, 1 tbsp dill seed, and ⅓ cup (100 g) salt in each. Remove the rubber bands from the lobsters and make sure the water is really boiling before placing them in the pots, two in each. Boil for 14 minutes and serve warm with clarified butter, grated horseradish, lemon, and dill.

Album tip: Grateful Dead *Live/Dead*
We just couldn't think of a more fitting
album, so there.

Whitefish roe with Västerbotten rösti,
citrusy red onion, and crème fraiche

🏁 WHITEFISH ROE WITH VÄSTERBOTTEN RÖSTI, CITRUSY RED ONION, AND CRÈME FRAICHE

Whitefish roe is among the tastiest we have in the shop and really you can just eat it as is. Some prefer blinis, but as you can see, we think a far more interesting combination looks like this. Just make sure you don't use too much Västerbotten cheese, as there is a risk it will dominate the flavors.

7–13 oz (200–400 g) white fish roe

Västerbotten Rösti
1.1 lbs (1 kg) potatoes, peeled and coarsely grated
½ cup (50 g) Västerbotten cheese, grated
½ cup (100 g) butter for frying
Salt and pepper

Squeeze as much water as possible from the potatoes. Mix the potatoes, cheese, salt, and pepper. Heat 4 small frying pans and divide half the butter between them. Place the potato mix in the pans and press down to make small cakes. Add more butter around the edges of the pans. Now press the edges of the cake inwards to create a round rösti. When the underside of the rösti feels firm and has a good color on the underside, it is ready to turn. Fry for 5 more minutes on medium heat.

Citrusy Red Onion
2 red onions, finely chopped
Juice of 1 lemon

Mix the red onion and lemon juice and leave to marinate for 30 minutes.

Crème Fraiche
1 cup (200 ml) crème fraiche
A good amount of black pepper

Mix the crème fraiche with the pepper. If it feels thin, mix it up with an electric whisk. It takes a while but give it a good, firm consistency.

Album tip: Rammstein *Mutter*
In light of the fact that rösti is a German
specialty, we couldn't miss the chance to
squeeze in Rammstein into this book.

Pollock fillet piccata with saffron risotto
and warm tomato salad

🚚 POLLOCK FILLET PICCATA WITH SAFFRON RISOTTO AND WARM TOMATO SALAD

The norm is to make a piccata using veal or pork, just like the Italians. However, we have discovered that you can just as easily use pollock fillets with a cheese batter. And if you really need to know, we can even reveal that this variety beats the original hands down.

Pollock

1.3 oz (600 g) pollock fillets
1⅔ cups (200 g) flour
2 eggs, whisked
2 cups (200 g) Parmesan, grated

Salt and white pepper
4 tbsp olive oil
2 tbsp butter
Salt and white pepper

Cut the fish into 8 pieces. Cover the pieces in flour, then the egg, and finally the Parmesan. Season with salt and white pepper. Fry the fish in oil and butter until golden brown.

Saffron Risotto

2 shallots, finely chopped
1 garlic clove, pressed
2 tbsp olive oil
1 cup (200 g) Arborio rice, or risotto rice
1 tsp (½ g) saffron

2¼ cups (500 ml) chicken stock
2 tbsp butter
½ cup (50 g) Parmesan, roughly grated
Salt and pepper

In a pan, fry the onion in the oil without giving it any color. Add the rice and saffron and fry one more minute, while stirring. Add half the stock and stir. Let the rice simmer on a low heat without a lid for 20 minutes, adding the rest of the stock gradually as it absorbs. When the risotto is ready (it should be slightly crunchy but cooked), add the Parmesan and butter. Season to taste with salt and pepper.

Album tip: Turbonegro
Apocalypse Dudes
As we couldn't think of any good albums from Italy, we took the first, best non-Italian record we could think of. It is likely, though, that Turbonegro has a large Italian fan club.

Tomato Salad

12 cherry tomatoes, halved
2 garlic cloves, sliced
4 tbsp olive oil
12 black olives

2 tbsp capers
1 bunch basil
½ cup (50 g) Parmesan, shaved

Fry the garlic in the oil until golden brown. Add the tomatoes, olives, capers, and stir quickly. Garnish with basil leaves and the shaved Parmesan.

Broiled scallops
with chorizo and pebre

BROILED SCALLOPS WITH CHORIZO AND PEBRE

Scallops are often present in rather meek dishes; in fact, dishes bordering on the boring side. Therefore we feel it is our duty to teach you a recipe with some bite, just the way it should be!

Scallops

12 scallops
2 tbsp cooking oil
2 chorizos
1 red pepper
1 red onion
2 avocadoes
1 green chili
1 tsp cilantro, and a few sprigs for garnish
1 lime
1 tbsp olive oil
Salt and white pepper

Finely dice the vegetables. Mix the zest and juice of the lime with the vegetables, add salt and pepper. Fry the chorizo and cut into 12 pieces. Season the scallops and fry in cooking oil on high heat for 30 seconds on each side.

Pebre

4 spring onions
2 tbsp fresh cilantro, chopped
2 chilis, seeded
1 vine tomato
1 tbsp tomato purée
1 garlic clove
2 tbsp red wine vinegar
2 tbsp olive oil
½ tsp pepper
Salt to taste

Mix the cilantro, spring onions, tomato, tomato purée, garlic, and chili in a blender. Add olive oil, vinegar, salt, and pepper.

Roast Potatoes

1.3 lbs (600 g) potatoes
3 tbsp olive oil
Salt
Crushed black pepper

Cut the potatoes in half and pour the oil over them. Season with salt and pepper and bake in the oven for about 25 minutes at 400°F (200°C).

Album tip: Fu Manchu *The Action Is Go*
Just as the title suggests, this record has some go in it. Our photographer Björn Tesch agrees, a classic!

Lobster spaghetti with funnel chanterelle,
squash, and artichoke

🦞🦞 LOBSTER SPAGHETTI WITH FUNNEL CHANTERELLE, SQUASH, AND ARTICHOKE

There are those that claim that pasta is something you throw together from leftovers found in the fridge. So if you have a couple of lobsters and some funnel chanterelles left over, and maybe a dash of cognac hanging around, we can teach you how to throw together the best pasta dish in the world.

2 boiled lobsters

Crack the lobsters and remove the meat from the claws and tail. Save the shell for the sauce. Warm the lobster meat in the sauce when it is time to eat.

Lobster Sauce

The lobster shell	¼ cup (50 ml) port
1 shallot, chopped	wine
½ carrot, diced	¼ cup (50 ml) cognac
¼ fennel, diced	2½ cups (500 ml)
2 tbsp cooking oil	cream
1 tbsp tomato purée	Salt and pepper
1 pinch ground paprika	

Roast the lobster shell and vegetables in the oil in a pan for 5–10 minutes. Add the spices, port wine, and cognac and reduce. Add the cream and simmer for 15 minutes. Take out and season to taste with salt and pepper.

Spaghetti

1 lb (400 g) spaghetti
½ cup (50 g) Parmesan, grated
The zest of 1 lemon
½ cup (50 g) arugula salad
Freshly ground black pepper

Cook and drain the spaghetti and mix with the Parmesan, lemon zest, arugula, and black pepper.

Sides

3 cups (300 g) butternut squash
1 Granny Smith apple
2 cups (100 g) funnel chanterelles
1 sprig flat leaf parsley, chopped
4 artichokes, cooked and separated
1 garlic clove
3 tbsp olive oil
Salt and black pepper

Peel and chop the apple and squash into cubes. Fry the squash in olive oil until soft and then add the mushrooms, apple, artichokes, parsley, and garlic. Season with salt and pepper.

Pasta Dough

1¼ cups (150 g) white flour	1 tbsp olive oil
	1 egg
1¼ cups (150 g) durum flour (you can use white flour as well)	2 egg yolks
	1 tbsp water
	1 pinch salt

Mix the ingredients together for a firm and smooth dough, kneading for around 10 minutes. Add more water if the dough feels hard. Let it rest for 1 hour in the fridge before using. Pass through a pasta machine to make the spaghetti.

Album tip: The Hellacopters *High Visibility*
According to rumors, The Hellacopters whisked together their
debut album in a few hours. This album may have taken a bit longer
to make but is based on the same principles as the debut.

Fried sole with lemon
potatoes and zucchini salad

45 FRIED SOLE WITH LEMON POTATOES AND ZUCCHINI SALAD

Sole is one of the less appreciated flatfish but one of the best when it comes to quality. If the sole were a share, it would be classed as undervalued.

Album tip: Kiss *Love Gun*
Okay, we admit that Gene
Simmons has a long tongue.
That's why we picked this
band. But *Love Gun* is also a
really good album, honestly!

8 lemon soles, 3 oz (75 g)
  each
1⅔ cups (200 g) flour

3 tbsp butter
¼ cup (50 ml) cooking oil
Salt and white pepper

Turn the fish fillets in the flour, season, and then fry in the butter and oil until golden brown.

Lemon Potatoes

1.3 lbs (600 g) peeled
  potatoes
Juice of 1 lemon
¼ cup (50 ml) water

⅓ cup (80 g) butter
1 bunch chives, chopped
Salt and white pepper

Boil the potatoes until tender and cut into pieces (they should still be warm). Place the potatoes in a pan, add water and the lemon juice, and bring to a boil. Add the butter while stirring and season to taste with salt and pepper. Finish by mixing in the chives.

Zucchini Salad

1 zucchini
1 bunch arugula, chopped
¼ cup (50 ml) sunflower seeds, roasted
2 tbsp olive oil
1 tsp white wine vinegar
Salt
Crushed black pepper

Cut the zucchini into long strips and mix with the rest of the ingredients.

Dill Pesto

1 pot of dill
½ cup (50 g) grated Västerbotten cheese
2 tbsp olive oil
2 tbsp blanched almonds
Salt and white pepper

Pick the dill from the stalks and mix together with the rest of the ingredients.

46

Warm salmon
with tempura

#6 WARM SALMON WITH TEMPURA

Does the quality of salmon matter? Actually, yes. Salma salmon is absolutely the best salmon there is and is carefully selected, filleted, and vacuum packed right after being caught. Does it taste different? You bet it does! In fact, it is so good, we think it is unnecessary to even cook it.

1 lb (400 g) Salma salmon (or best quality salmon available)
4 tbsp grated ginger
4 tbsp grated radish

Cut the salmon into thin slices and put on plates. Pour the warm dipping sauce over the salmon when serving. Serve with the ginger and radish, vegetables, and cold dipping sauce.

Vegetables
Fresh vegetables, for example:
12 green asparagus
1 bunch carrots
12 spring onions
1 zucchini cut into long sticks
2 cups (100 g) shiitake mushrooms

Tempura batter
¾ cup (100 g) corn flour
3¼ cups (400 g) flour
4 egg yolks
2¼ cups (500 ml) cold water
2 pinches salt

Mix the ingredients into a batter (mix the batter as little as possible).

2¼–3 cups (500–700 ml) cooking oil for frying
Heat the oil to 310–325°F (160–170°C). Dip the vegetables in the tempura batter and deep fry until golden brown in the warm oil. Remove the vegetables and allow the fat to drain on paper towels.

Dipping Sauce
½ cup (100 ml) soy sauce
½ cup (100 ml) mirin, Japanese wine
3 tbsp sake
1 tbsp granulated sugar
1 tbsp rice wine vinegar

Mix the ingredients and bring to a boil. Let the sauce boil for 5 minutes and then leave it to cool. Pour the sauce into small dipping bowls and reserve ½ cup (100 ml) to heat up and pour over the salmon.

Album tip: Iggy & The Stooges *Raw Power*
Never has the name of an album been more fitting. Music, packaging, and fish in perfect symbiosis.

Fried cod with pumpkin purée
and shallots in red wine

FRIED COD WITH PUMPKIN PURÉE AND SHALLOTS IN RED WINE

It's hard to imagine that there was a time when cod was considered inferior. You can't help but feel sorry for the fish in question, so this recipe is our way to give it some retribution.

The Fish
4 pieces of cod, 6 oz (180 g) each
1 tbsp salt
1 quart (1 liter) water

Mix the salt and water and add the cod, letting it lightly
marinate for an hour. Remove the cod pieces and dry them
off with kitchen roll. Fry in the olive oil at a medium heat.

The Vegetables
2¼ cups (150 g) button mushrooms
4 root parsleys, peeled and divided lengthwise
2 fresh garlic, in cloves
A few sprigs of thyme
½ cup (100 ml) olive oil
Salt and white pepper

Place the vegetables on a baking tray together with the squash purée
(below). Add olive oil and season with salt, pepper, and the thyme.
Bake for 25 minutes at 400°F (200°C).

Squash Purée
1.3 lbs (600 g) butternut squash, peeled and diced
4 tbsp crème fraiche
2 tbsp olive oil
Salt and white pepper
Water

Purée the pumpkin with the crème fraiche, olive oil, and a little water if
needed. Season to taste with salt and pepper.

Shallots in Red Wine
8 shallots
½ cup (100 ml) balsamic vinegar
½ cup (100 ml) red wine
2 tsp granulated sugar
1 tbsp butter
Salt and white pepper

Peel and slice the onion into rings. Mix with the rest
of the ingredients and boil until all the liquid has
evaporated. Season to taste with salt and pepper.

Album tip: Weezer's blue album
College pop with distorted guitars that turned rock and roll
upside down in the mid '90s. The revenge of the nerds!

Moules frites with aioli

48 MOULES FRITES WITH AIOLI

We have discussed it for years, running a bistro that only sells moules frites.
Forget everything else—if people come, it is because there will be mussels and fries.
The question is not if, but when, just wait and see.

Aioli
3 garlic cloves
3 egg yolks
½ cup (100 ml) cooking oil
¼ cup (50 ml) olive oil
½ tsp salt
2 tbsp lemon juice

Place the garlic, egg yolks, lemon juice, and
salt in a food processor. Add the oil in a thin
drizzle until the sauce thickens.

Moules Frites

1.1 lbs (½ kg) potatoes, cut into ½ inch
(1 cm) thick sticks and rinsed in cold water
2.2 lbs (1 kg) blue mussels
1 banana shallot, chopped
2 garlic cloves, chopped
1 tbsp olive oil
1¼ cups (300 ml) white wine
¼ cup (50 g) butter
½ cup (50 g) parsley, chopped
Salt and pepper

Place the potato sticks on a kitchen towel to dry. Clean and polish the mussels. Start frying the potatoes and fry the onion and garlic in the olive oil. Add the mussels and wine and cook for 3 minutes. Remove the mussels with a slotted spoon and place in a bowl. Add butter and parsley to the wine stock and mix with a handheld mixer, adding salt and pepper to taste. Pour the stock over the mussels and place the French fries on the side.

Mussels and French fries, man that's good . . .

Album tip: Rage Against the Machine, the first album.
We discussed playing *only* Rage Against the Machine at our restaurant; in the kitchen, that is.

Crayfish gratin
with focaccia bread

49 CRAYFISH GRATIN WITH FOCACCIA BREAD

Very Italian and very easy once you are done with the bread. It's simply a question of halving the crayfish, adding the rest of the ingredients, and putting it in the oven. Then you can serve the whole pot and dip the bread straight into the melted butter. Tremendously tasty in all its simplicity.

Crayfish

16 raw crayfish
1¼ cups (300 g) butter at room temperature
2 garlic cloves
2 egg yolks
½ pot of oregano, chopped
16 cocktail tomatoes
½ cup (100 g) black olives
½ cup (100 g) green olives
½ pot of oregano, sprigs
Salt and black pepper

Divide the crayfish lengthwise and place the halves, meat side up, in an oven-proof dish. Whisk butter, egg yolks, and oregano. Place a tablespoon of the butter on top of each crayfish and add the olives, tomatoes, salt, and pepper. Bake in the oven for 7–10 minutes at 435°F (225°C). Sprinkle with oregano sprigs and serve with freshly baked focaccia.

Focaccia

2 tbsp (30 g) yeast
1¼ cups (300 ml) lukewarm water
3¾ cups (450 g) flour
1 tbsp olive oil
1 pinch salt
½ cup (100 g) black and green olives
1 garlic clove
2 tbsp olive oil
1 sprig rosemary

Dissolve the yeast in the water and add the flour, olive oil, and salt. Mix to form a dough and proof under a paper towel for 30 minutes. Spread the dough onto an oiled baking tray and proof for another 30 minutes. Make small pockets in the dough and insert the olives. Crush the garlic into the remaining olive oil and brush the bread with the garlic oil. Sprinkle some rosemary and some coarse salt on top. Bake the bread for 15–20 minutes at 425°F (220°C). Cool on a rack.

Cod with green lentils, soured red cabbage,
and garlic reduction sauce

50 COD WITH GREEN LENTILS, SOURED RED CABBAGE, AND GARLIC REDUCTION SAUCE

Which fish dish should you focus on before the worst of the Christmas hysteria begins? Cod of course! If you choose this recipe you will also get the chance to pre-eat some red cabbage, just to get used to the idea before everything ends up tasting like cinnamon. If you can get your hands on puy lentils, buy these instead of the green lentils for the recipe. They taste better and are more attractive.

The Cod
2 lbs (900 g) whole cod, divided into four pieces
4 garlic cloves, lightly crushed
10 sprigs of wild thyme
½ cup (100 g) butter
½ cup (100 ml) fish stock
½ cup (100 ml) chicken stock
Salt and black pepper

Place half the butter in a frying pan on medium heat. Season the fish before frying it together with the garlic and thyme. Fry for 4–5 minutes on one side, then turn and baste with the butter. Add the rest of the butter and fry for 4 more minutes. Keep basting the fish to spread the flavor. Remove the hake and add the chicken and fish stock to the pan. Allow to cook for a few minutes so that the sauce divides between stock on the bottom and fat on top. Pour some of this freshly made reduction over the fish.

Green Lentils
1½ cups (300 g) green lentils, dried
½ shallot, chopped
1 garlic clove
2¼ cups (500 ml) fish stock
2 tbsp lemon juice
2 pots of parsley
1 tbsp olive oil
2 tbsp butter
Salt and pepper

Boil the lentils in the stock together with the onion and garlic. Let it simmer under a lid for around 20 minutes (there should be a little bite still in the lentils). If there is not enough liquid, you can add some water, but only just enough to cover the lentils. Mix the parsley with the oil and lemon until you have a green purée. Pour out some of the liquid from the lentils until a third remains. Add the butter and parsley mixture and cook until you have a mushy consistency. Season with salt and pepper.

Soured Red Cabbage
1½ cups (150 g) red cabbage finely cut into strips
1 tbsp cooking oil
2 tbsp sugar
2 tbsp red wine vinegar
Salt and pepper

Heat a frying pan. Add the oil and let the sugar melt in the pan. Add the cabbage and swirl it around the pan to warm it. Add the vinegar, salt, and pepper and serve immediately. Please note that the whole process should take 30 seconds.

Album tip: Soundgarden *Superunknown*
"Black Hole Sun" and "Spoonman" in all their
glory, but also taste a track like "Limo Wreck."

Herring and Atlantic herring

We hardly need to tell you that homemade herring tastes better than store-bought herring from a jar. It is worth noting though that the herring needs to be left for a while, a bit like chip dips, to taste really good. Therefore always start the pickling process at least 24 hours before the herring is to be eaten. If you want it to taste really good, buy herring imported from Iceland and ferment it in white vinegar for 3–4 days.

Herring in Mustard Sauce

3 fillets of herring, pickled and cut into pieces
3 tbsp Swedish mustard
1 tbsp white wine vinegar
2 tbsp granulated sugar
½ cup (100 ml) cooking oil
1 pinch white pepper
1 tbsp cognac
2 tbsp dill, chopped

Mix the mustard, sugar, and vinegar. Add the oil gradually, drop by drop. Add cognac, white pepper, and dill. Marinate the herring in this mixture for at least 12 hours.

Old Man's Herring

3 herring fillets, pickled and cut into pieces
1 egg, hard boiled and chopped
½ yellow onion, finely chopped
15 straws of chive, chopped
1 tbsp dill, chopped
1 tbsp white fish roe
¼ cup (50 g) sour cream
½ cup (100 g) mayonnaise
Salt and white pepper

Mix all the ingredients and season to taste.

Vodka Lime Herring

3 herring fillets, drained
3 tbsp white vinegar
2 tbsp lime juice
⅓ cup (100 g) sugar
½ cup (125 ml) water
5 white peppercorns
5 cloves
2 tbsp vodka

In a skillet, mix sugar, water, lime juice, white pepper, and cloves, and cook until it boils. Take off the heat and add the vinegar and vodka. Allow to cool. Add the herring to the marinade and leave for at least 24 hours.

Herrings in Sherry

3 Atlantic herrings cut into 1 inch (2 cm) pieces
½ cup (100 g) tomato purée
¼ cup (50 ml) red wine vinegar
¼ cup (50 g) sugar
¼ cup (50 ml) cooking oil
2 tbsp sherry
1 red onion, finely shredded
2 bay leaves, crushed
8 white peppercorns, crushed

Mix tomato purée, sugar, and vinegar. Carefully add the oil. Mix the rest of the ingredients. Set aside for at least 6 hours.

Pickled Herring

9 herring fillets, drained
½ cup (100 ml) white vinegar
¾ cup (200 g) sugar
1¼ cups (300 ml) water
2 red onions, roughly chopped
2½ inches (6 cm) leek, roughly
    chopped
1 small carrot, peeled
10 allspice corns
2 bay leaves
5 cloves

Boil sugar, water, vegetables, and spices. When brought to a boil, remove from the heat and add the white vinegar. Allow to cool. Run the marinade through a sieve and pour over the herrings. Set aside for at least 24 hours. Cut the herring fillets into pieces and garnish with the red onion when serving.

Marinated Atlantic Herring

1.3 lbs (600 g) fillets of Atlantic herring
2¼ cups (500 ml) water
½ cup (100 ml) white vinegar
1 tbsp salt

Remove the skin from the fillets starting at the head and pulling back. Mix water, white vinegar, and salt and place the fillets in the marinade for 12 hours. Turn every four hours to marinate evenly.

Atlantic Herring Marinated with White Fish Roe

11 oz (300 g) Atlantic herring fillets, marinated
½ cup (100 g) sour cream
½ cup (100 g) mayonnaise
2 tbsp white fish roe
1 tbsp dill, chopped
Salt and white pepper

Mix together all the ingredients and season to taste with the salt and white pepper.

Spice, Onion, and Dill Atlantic Herring

10.5 oz (300 wg)
    marinated fillets
    of Atlantic herring
¾ cup (200 g) sugar
1 yellow onion, chopped
1 red onion, chopped
1 tbsp lemon pepper
2 tbsp allspice, crushed
1 tbsp white pepper, crushed
1 bay leaf crushed
2 tbsp dill, chopped

Mix together all the ingredients and set aside for at least 48 hours.

Album tips: Them Crooked Vultures, Josh Homme (Queens Of The Stone Age, Kyuss), Dave Grohl (Nirvana, Foo Fighters) and John Paul Jones (Led Zeppelin). Quality music for connoisseurs.

Canapés

Take a break the day before New Year's Eve. Joking aside, canapés can be a headache if you get them wrong. Prepare all the ingredients in advance so that they are prepped and ready to go in the fridge. Then all you have to do is bring them out and lay out the components in the right order. Kind of like a building set or a puzzle.

King Crab with Avruga Caviar

1 slice of bread
½ a leg of king crab
1 tbsp avruga caviar
Butter

Using a cookie cutter with a 1-inch (3 cm) diameter, cut out 4 shapes from the bread. Butter the bread. Slice the crab and place the crab and caviar on top of the bread.

Asian Tuna Tartar

1 slice of thin white bread
3.5 oz (100 g) fresh tuna, finely chopped
1 tbsp soy sauce
½ tsp wasabi
2 tbsp sesame seeds, roasted
4 quail egg yolks

Using a cookie cutter, cut 4 shapes from the bread and bake in the oven until crispy. Mix the tuna with the soy sauce and wasabi. Shape the tuna into four puck-shaped circles and roll in the sesame seeds. Place the tuna on the bread and top off with an egg yolk on each.

White Fish Roe

1 slice white bread
Butter
3 oz (80 g) white fish roe
1 tsp crème fraiche
4 arches of red onion

Using a cookie cutter with a 1-inch (3 cm) diameter, cut 4 shapes from the bread. Butter the bread and divide the roe between them. Garnish with crème fraiche and red onion.

Cold Smoked Salmon and Pickles

1 slice bread
4 small slices cold smoked salmon
2½ inch (6 cm) pickle, thinly sliced
1 tbsp white vinegar
2 tbsp sugar
3 tbsp water
Butter
Watercress

Mix the vinegar, sugar, and water. Add the pickle and leave for 15 minutes. Using a cookie cutter with a 1 inch (3 cm) diameter, cut 4 shapes from the bread. Butter the bread and add the salmon and pickle. Garnish with the watercress.

Tacos with Scallops

1 wheat tortilla
2 scallops, chopped
¼ of a red chili
3 chive straws, chopped
1 tbsp trout roe
Sunflower greens
Salt and black pepper
Oil for frying

Using a cookie cutter with a 2-inch (5 cm) diameter, cut 4 shapes from the tortilla. Fold each tortilla circle with metal tweezers and carefully fry until crispy. Mix the scallops with the chili and chives, and season to taste with the salt and pepper. Place the sunflower greens at the bottom of the "taco shell," add the scallops, and finish off with some trout roe.

Shrimp with Truffle Mayonnaise and Quail Eggs

1 slice white bread
Butter
20 shrimp, peeled
1 tbsp good quality mayonnaise
1 drop truffle oil
1 quail egg
Dill

Using a cookie cutter with a 1½-inch (4 cm) diameter, cut 4 shapes from the bread. Butter the bread and layer the shrimp on top. Mix the mayonnaise and the oil and add to the shrimp. Boil the quail egg for 3 minutes and cool quickly. Slice the egg and top the canapé with egg and dill.

Album tip: Sex Pistols *The Great Rock 'n' Roll Swindle*
Apart from the symphony version of "God Save the Queen" and "EMI," it offers the Sid Vicious rendition of "My Way." In other words, it is perfect for a cocktail party.

Real Caviar

1–4 jars of caviar (the highest quality you can afford)
1 caviar spoon

Place the caviar on the spoon and rest it in your hand. Eat and enjoy . . .

Lobster with Avocado, Tomato, and Truffle

1 slice bread
Butter
1 lobster tail, sliced
¼ of avocado, pitted and neatly sliced
¼ of tomato, seeded and carefully sliced
Salt and pepper
1 slice black truffle, shredded

Remove the crusts from the bread and divide into four rectangular pieces around 1 x 1½ inches (3 x 4 cm) each. Butter the bread and add salt and pepper to the tomato and avocado. Layer the lobster meat with the tomato and avocado and finish off with the truffle.

RECIPE INDEX

Perfect, you have now eaten your way through fifty-two weeks of the year.

No?

We guessed as much. But hopefully the recipes you have tried have given you a taste to try some more. In that case, we have succeeded with what we set out to do: helping you discover the delicacies of the sea, as well as some classic tunes.

If you have opinions about the recipes, music choice, or the drinks, don't hesitate to contact us at our seafood restaurant Hav (Sea) in Hötorgshallen, Stockholm.

Last but not least, thanks for choosing our book, we hope you enjoyed it.

First published by Norstedts, Sweden, in 2012, as *Hav* by Pär-Anders Bergqvist and Anders Engvall. Published by agreement with Norstedts Agency.

Concept, design and production: Holy Diver
Text: Pär-Anders Bergqvist, Anders Engvall & Holy Diver
Photographer: Björn Tesch
Sea photos: Björn Tesch, p. 72, 108, 128, 138, 140, 144, 160
Other sea photos: Shutterstock
Thanks to: Petter Toen

Skyhorse Publishing books may be purchased in bulk at special discounts for sales promotion, corporate gifts, fund-raising, or educational purposes. Special editions can also be created to specifications. For details, contact the Special Sales Department, Skyhorse Publishing, 307 West 36th Street, 11th Floor, New York, NY 10018 or info@skyhorsepublishing.com.

Skyhorse® and Skyhorse Publishing® are registered trademarks of Skyhorse Publishing, Inc.®, a Delaware corporation.

www.skyhorsepublishing.com

10 9 8 7 6 5 4 3 2 1

Library of Congress Cataloging-in-Publication Data is available on file.

ISBN: 978-1-62087-733-3

Printed in China